"Dr. Brenda takes the gloves off to teach the next generation of reconcilers how, like Nehemiah, to repair the compromised walls of God's church for the ongoing, holy work of racial and structural healing. It's her bravest, most urgent, and wise, yet hopeful and strategic, guide and pronouncement to date. An inspiring triumph."

—**Patricia Raybon**, Christy Award–winning author of the books *My First White Friend*, *I Told the Mountain to Move*, and the Annalee Spain Mysteries

"McNeil is one of the most important scholars and practitioners of racial reconciliation of our generation. This book offers a new paradigm for thinking about the work of reconciliation at this heartbreaking moment. It is timely, powerful, and so very necessary. It must make its way into the hands of every pastor, congregant, and Christian who believes there is a work of reconciliation yet to be done."

—**Willie James Jennings**, Yale Divinity School

"*Empowered to Repair* is the sum of sage wisdom from a lifelong reconciler. Through story and precept Dr. Brenda shares what must be done here and now, why, how to do it, and how to take care of ourselves and our communities while on the reconciliation journey. While every chapter contains valuable knowledge and guidance, the chapter on reparations is worth the price of admission. For those awaiting the tools to make a better world, you found them!"

—**Rev. Randy Woodley**, author, speaker, co-sustainer: Eloheh Indigenous Center for Earth Justice

"Beginning with the challenging observation that the Christian reconciliation movement has lost its power because of a failure to do the work of repair, McNeil describes an ongoing spiritual process that leads to reparative action. This process can take place (by God's grace) on a personal level or on a collective level, but either way, the culminating question is, 'What can I do to make it right?' As I finished reading this challenging and richly nuanced work, I found myself praying that God would give each of us the strength to participate fully in the ministry of reconciliation by asking this question and then doing it."

—**Ruth Haley Barton**, founder, Transforming Center; author of *Strengthening the Soul of Your Leadership*

"Many people know Dr. Brenda as an incredible preacher and inspiring communicator. *Empowered to Repair* reveals that this wise and passionate reconciliation leader is also a skilled strategist. Are you weary of conversations and debates about justice? Are you ready to practically and meaningfully contribute to systemic healing in your community? Good news—you're holding the playbook in your hands. Let's get to work!"

—**David Swanson**, pastor, New Community Covenant Church; CEO of New Community Outreach

"The work of reconciliation is ultimately a work of love. Having done this work of love for many decades, Dr. Brenda generously offers the wisdom she has gained along the way as a gift to her readers. In an increasingly polarized and hostile world, Dr. Brenda calls the people of God out of our places of comfort and into places of dissonance to embody God's love and justice for the world as our faithful response to God's call."

—**Julie Tai**, Fuller Theological Seminary; cofounder of Kinship Commons

"For emerging Christian leaders wanting to walk the path of justice, this book is a great guide for the journey. Drawing from the life and narrative of Nehemiah, it illuminates important thematic signposts like lament, proximity, prayer, self-care, and reparations, all of which are vital to justice."

—**Robert Chao Romero**, UCLA Chavez Department of Chicana/o and Central American Studies; author of *Brown Church*

"With years of hard-earned wisdom gained from close proximity to the challenges, Dr. Brenda injects new-generation paradigms and relevant practical advice into her biblically rooted vision of reconciliation. This book will inspire and instruct readers on their own journey as instruments of healing and as activists for reconciliation."

—**Curtiss Paul DeYoung**, Co-CEO, Minnesota Council of Churches

"McNeil explains why the church in the United States has lost its witness and invites us to repair it so that the church can be an inclusive community known for the love it embodies. For those who grieve the church's witness and are committed to reconciliation, this is the book to read to take the necessary steps toward mending what has been broken."

—**Jennifer Guerra Aldana**, Point Loma Nazarene University; cofounder of Kinship Commons

"In *Empowered to Repair*, Dr. Brenda reminds us why her work is indispensable: because she lives out the teachings of her text. In encouraging the church to move toward concrete action, Dr. Brenda not only speaks and teaches biblical truth, she also demonstrates it. This book points the church toward a possible brighter future as a reconciled church—a message we so desperately need to heed."

—**Soong-Chan Rah**, Fuller Theological Seminary

"*Empowered to Repair* presses further into making the ministry of reconciliation tangible, organized, and sustainable. Activating communities for transformative change is challenging work, so Dr. Brenda invites the reader into the biblical narrative of Nehemiah and the grassroots realities of structural injustice. I can think of no better person to lead this journey. I have witnessed Dr. Brenda at work, and this book continues her legacy as a faithful voice of courage, hope, and love."

—**David Leong**, Seattle Pacific University and Seminary

EMPOWERED TO REPAIR

Previous Books by Author

*Becoming Brave: Finding the Courage to Pursue
Racial Justice Now*

*Roadmap to Reconciliation 2.0: Moving
Communities into Unity, Wholeness and Justice*

*A Credible Witness: Reflections on Power, Evangelism
and Race*

*The Heart of Racial Justice: How Soul Change Leads
to Social Change* (coauthored by Rick Richardson)

EMPOWERED
TO REPAIR

BECOMING PEOPLE WHO MEND BROKEN SYSTEMS
AND HEAL OUR COMMUNITIES

BRENDA SALTER McNEIL

BrazosPress

a division of Baker Publishing Group
Grand Rapids, Michigan

Published by Brazos Press
a division of Baker Publishing Group
Grand Rapids, Michigan
BrazosPress.com

Printed in the United States of America

Library of Congress Cataloging-in-Publication Data
Names: McNeil, Brenda Salter, 1955– author.
Title: Empowered to repair : becoming people who mend broken systems and heal our communities / Brenda Salter McNeil.
Description: Grand Rapids, Michigan : Brazos Press, a division of Baker Publishing Group, [2024] | Includes bibliographical references.
Identifiers: LCCN 2023049272 | ISBN 9781587434488 (cloth) | ISBN 9781493438594 (ebook) | ISBN 9781493438600 (pdf)
Subjects: LCSH: Reconciliation—Religious aspects—Christianity. | Race discrimination—Religious aspects—Christianity. | Bible. Nehemiah—Commentaries.
Classification: LCC BT738.27 .M35 2024 | DDC 222/.806—dc23/eng/20240110
LC record available at https://lccn.loc.gov/2023049272

Unless otherwise indicated, Scripture quotations are from the Common English Bible. © Copyright 2011 by the Common English Bible. All rights reserved. Used by permission.

Scripture quotations labeled NRSV are taken from the New Revised Standard Version Updated Edition. Copyright © 2021 National Council of Churches of Christ in the United States of America. Used by permission. All rights reserved worldwide.

Cover design by Matthew Lewis

The Author is represented by Alive Literary Agency, www.aliveliterary.com.

Baker Publishing Group publications use paper produced from sustainable forestry practices and postconsumer waste whenever possible.

24   25   26   27   28   29   30   7   6   5   4   3   2   1

In honor of my mentors in
the ministry of reconciliation,
who have laid the foundation:

Dr. William (Bill) Pannell
Dr. Tony Campolo
Dr. John M. Perkins
Dr. Ray Bakke

And to my children,
Omari and Mia,
who continually inspire me
to envision a better future

Your ancient ruins shall be rebuilt;
  you shall raise up the foundations of many
    generations;
you shall be called the repairer of the breach,
  the restorer of streets to live in.

Isaiah 58:12 (NRSV)

Contents

Preface

We are always left saddened but not shocked. This will happen again. Another black queen or king, doing what should be considered a regular activity, will be killed—just because. Black people will express outrage, while everyone else will continue on, relatively unchanged. We'll exclaim, #BlackLivesMatter, and we will get countless comments about "what about All Lives Matter"—I'm looking at you White Evangelical churches. The shock will wear off for the rest of the world, and we'll be left to rebuild again . . . by ourselves. This cycle is so engrained in the black American narrative that we have learned to quickly spring into actionable next steps because we've done this before and will do it again. We've had no choice but to normalize the trauma and carry on. So, to those who wonder—I have no hope that I, or my future children will ever live in a world that is "equal," "totally safe," or "fair"—even though I will always fight for it. Sadly, for me and so many others, I lost that dream as a little boy.[1]

My dear son, Omari, wrote this on Facebook after the tragic death of Ahmaud Arbery, a twenty-five-year-old Black man who was chased while jogging and murdered by three white men in a South Georgia neighborhood. The truth and transparency of my son's words made me weep. We are indeed living in a world that is more divided than ever, and yet followers of Jesus are significantly absent in addressing the social injustice and divisiveness in our world. Christians are perceived as being absent from the work of addressing systemic and structural inequities. Consequently, Christians have little credibility when promoting justice and social change, especially among the next generation of young people who are fighting for their lives.

This deeply concerns me, because for almost forty years I have devoted my life to working for reconciliation. In that time, I've seen the level of racial, social, political, and global divisiveness escalate to what seems like an all-time high. In response to these deep divisions, dedicated and competent reconciliation leaders have made valiant attempts to build bridges to a different way forward that brings healing. Yet these global, national, and cultural rifts are so deeply entrenched that even leaders' best efforts for reconciliation are proving to be ineffective.

We are living in a time when the walls of our democracy, accountability, credibility, and civility—the foundations of a healthy, flourishing society—are crumbling all around us. Where there was once a standard of integrity, trustworthiness, and truth, there is now an expectation of lies and corruption from political and religious leaders. Prominent people in the media and business worlds commit blatant offenses without fear of reprimand or liability. Our judicial system of checks and balances has been hijacked by money and power. Amid this, a majority of Christians have lost the moral authority to confront these urgent issues because of their lack of action and their complicity in the face of this destruction. Far too many people of faith are watching the walls of a healthy society come down, with little vision or motivation to repair them.

From my vantage, the Christian reconciliation movement has lost its power to mobilize change. This became clear to me in a conversation with Troy Jackson, the cofounder of Living UNDIVIDED, which provides training for churches and faith-based organizations to help them explore the intersection of faith and race. We talked about our many years working with churches and consulting with Christian colleges and organizations to enable them to implement reconciliation in their ministry contexts. Troy asked me to describe the various stages of my reconciliation model and what each phase entails. I briefly explained the process, beginning with *catalytic events* that trigger the need for reconciliation. Some people will react by retreating into a cycle of *isolation and preservation* to maintain the status quo. However, people of color and those on the front lines fighting for reconciliation and equity may need to enter the *restoration cycle* to renew, recharge, and reconnect with God, themselves, and their community.

As I continued to describe the model, I explained that the reconciliation process starts with *realization*, discovering a new reality. *Identification* comes next, leading to finding commonalities with diverse people and understanding that "your people are my people." In the *preparation* phase, groups develop policies and procedures to support lasting change throughout the church or organization. *Activation* is the final phase, where Christians work with those in their local community to repair broken systems of injustice. After my explanation, Troy leaned toward me and asked, "How many of them have actually gotten into the activation phase?" I thought of the churches and colleges I've worked with and couldn't think of *one* that was actively working to fix systems of injustice.

Troy said, "I think we need to get people into activation earlier." I absolutely agreed.

Over the past few years, I've become convinced that we need a new paradigm that clarifies what Christians must do to actively engage in the work of reconciliation. The next generation of emerging reconciliation leaders is desperately seeking to be equipped so they can effectively respond to the deeply embedded divisions where they live, work, and serve. They want to know how to lead people to a transformed reality that's defined by health and wholeness. One of my students, David Gardinier, made this clear to me before he graduated from Seattle Pacific University. I'll never forget the day when David said to me in class, "Dr. B, we don't want any more theory! We've read the books about history, sociology, and theology. Now we need to know what to do! How do we keep from becoming part of the problem and work to be part of the solution?" He went on to say, "For example, when we graduate and move to another city, what is the first thing we should do to advocate for reconciliation?" That was a challenging conversation that forced me to reexamine my pedagogy and curriculum. As a result, I began using a narrative and experiential learning approach that led me to the biblical book of Nehemiah.

In the biblical narrative of Nehemiah, we see reconciliation in action as well as a spiritual, ethical, and practical framework for engaging reconciliation and reparations in ways that can transform broken relationships and systems. I believe this book is a guide for organizing, empowering, and activating people to join in God's work of reconciliation in their local context. It leads us through a progressive process of questioning, lamenting, praying, surveying, identifying, strategizing, and establishing supportive structures that enable people to use their resources and to empower communities to work together for the common good. Nehemiah moves Christians beyond extending "thoughts and prayers" or lamenting about the horrible violence and racial injustice happening all around us. Instead, the story of Nehemiah shows us what it looks like to address the problem by mobilizing people to get actively involved.

In addition to the biblical narrative, we will explore the spiritual and prophetic work needed to address racial and social injustice in our local context and surrounding community. We will also take an honest look at how Black, Indigenous, and people of color (BIPOC), on the one hand, and those who are white, on the other, have different needs and need to do disparate work to repair what is broken. In addition, we'll discover strategies to make systemic changes that go beyond superficial relational diversity. Finally, we'll clearly identify the skills needed to engage in this work as a marathon requiring deep rest, community, and transformational prayer.

In essence, I'm writing this book to answer David's question: *How do we keep from becoming part of the problem and work to be part of the solution?* I want to give the next generation practical principles for how to actively work for reconciliation. I hope this book will embolden and empower them to work with others in their communities to cocreate a new way forward. I'm convinced that the next generation of Christian leaders is poised to bridge the credibility gap between people committed to Jesus who are working for justice and those committed to Jesus who are not engaged in this struggle. Many reconciliation leaders are involved in their own efforts within their various spheres of influence, but I believe we are stronger together. This means we must break out of our silos to work for our collective healing. To do this, we will have to come together with others to honestly assess why faith-based communities have lost their ability to influence social change.

I look forward to journeying with you and I hope you will gain insights and practical principles for working with others to cultivate a better future. I pray that this book will inform and empower you to actively work to repair broken relationships and systems through collective action. As Christians, we must stop talking about reconciliation and actually do something to demonstrate that we care. We must show up in the places where our solidarity and support are most needed. We must learn new strategies to mobilize people so they can help rebuild and restore communities where all people and creation can flourish. If we are to regain our credibility as Christians with the next generation, we have to give feet to our prayers and address the social problems around us. Even if we don't succeed, we have to *do* something to become part of the solution. The adage is true: our actions speak louder than our words.

Introduction

I was thirteen years old when Martin Luther King Jr. was assassinated. It terrified me to watch enraged protestors smashing windows one moment, then being corralled like animals by the police the next. The usual calm darkness of night was disrupted by flames shooting up into the night sky, identifying where buildings and cars were on fire. Although my family and I admired King from afar and were devastated by his death, I wasn't raised to be protesting in the streets.

As a young Black girl from a working-class family with middle-class values on the East Coast, I was raised to respect my parents, go to church, get good grades, and eventually go to college. My two Black parents also had a keen understanding about the potentially mortal danger of a Black child engaging in any activity, no matter how justified, that would result in a possible encounter with the police. So, in their patience and wisdom, I joined my pain and outrage with that of the crowds from the safety and distance of my second-floor bedroom window.

It wasn't until college that the gap between observer and participant began to close for me. I became a follower of Jesus and made a sincere decision to allow my faith to change my life. But for many years, my faith was disconnected from any sort of social action or pursuit of justice. I understood that deep spirituality and political activism were critical for leaders like Martin Luther King Jr., but I didn't think I had any duty or obligation to act. I thought he was an exceptional man of great faith and commitment, but I was content to remain in my faith bubble. It wasn't until many years later that I knew I was called to do more than observe.

My inactivity was not unique then, nor is it unusual now. There is a common misconception that faith-based social activism is limited to those few gifted leaders such as King. As a result, many Christians excuse themselves from participation in activities or conversations to confront or challenge the social injustice and racial inequities taking place all around us. There is still a perception that the work of reconciliation is for others. Many Christians choose to watch from their church pews or living room couches or kitchen tables. Few enter the fight.

This silence has given place to the rise of racism, hatred, misogyny, homophobia, and injustice like we have not seen in decades. Those who have spoken, the loudest ones, have only made it worse. They stoke the flames of hate speech, harmful actions, and divisive ideologies. As a result, this generation is watching the conflation of Christianity and white evangelical nationalism.

I am convinced that the remedy will demand a radical shift in how we understand and embody the church. This generation of young adults wants justice and inclusion that results from real systemic change. Being a multiethnic community is not their goal. They want to move beyond numerical diversity, instead working for the healing and repairing of racialized social systems. This involves collaborative decision-making where everyone is represented and invited to cocreate policies and systems that empower everyone to be treated equitably. Young Christian leaders know they must do things differently than their predecessors. They are keenly aware that old methods will not work to solve the complex challenges and realities they face. They know the world is shifting and their global reality demands they take a new perspective and an innovative approach.

For this group of young Christian leaders, graduate school may not be the most helpful way to lead people out of our polarized and divisive sociopolitical environment. Instead, they might look elsewhere for people who are more proximate to systemic injustice and know its tangible impact on real people's lives. The ability to move in a new direction will require Christians to take the risk of following leaders who are different from what is traditional or familiar. We may need to ask new questions, such as:

- If we believe that God can speak to all of us, do we believe God is speaking through other people who don't look, think, or sound like us?
- Do we believe God shows up and speaks truth through those who don't have access to education in the ways we expect or deem necessary?

My experiences have taught me that the revelation of God often comes through our interaction with those who are challenging the status quo and our own norms. Interacting with those who break the status quo can inspire us to get actively involved in meaningful ways. Maybe this new thing that God is doing is being led by those who know how to organize and mobilize people to work together to achieve real change, and seminary training is of less import. These are the voices we should listen to and acknowledge by saying, "We recognize that God is moving in your generation in ways we did not see or anticipate. What you hear and are calling us to do is more than we expected. But your truth is prophetic. Through your justified anger, passion, and righteous indignation, God is speaking to us, and we need to listen to you because your voice matters!" Understandably, this posture of openness to a new way forward will challenge our understanding of the church.

For years I've been preaching and writing about the need for the church to create new wineskins. I've come to realize that when God pours out new wine, it often catches us by surprise. I can still vividly remember the shock I felt while having dinner with friends as we talked about the need to activate reconciliation in local churches and communities. During our conversation, in the quiet of my heart, I heard the Spirit say, "If you're looking for something new, you have to look outside the church." I thought to myself, "What! Is God telling me—a churchy Christian—to look outside the church?"

I had to grapple with my inaccurate thinking about the concept of the church. When I told a dear friend that God was calling me to look outside the church, she asked, "Is the church a noun or a verb?" Her question left me speechless. I realized that many people discuss "church" as if it's a noun—a place to go, like inside a box. My friend's question caused me to reconsider whether church is a place we go on Sundays or a verb we can experience anytime we choose.

After reflection, I determined that the church is not a building or a gathering in a particular place. Instead, we are the ecclesia, which in the original Greek means "the called-out ones." The church contains the called-out people of God wherever we live, work, or serve. Christ is not trapped in a building. Perhaps God is inviting us to reimagine the church as something bigger and more active than the boxes we've created. God may indeed be calling us to look outside our limited misperceptions so we can experience the dynamic reality of what it means to be the called-out ones.

For too many people, church is a restricting place rather than an expansive space. Therefore, many young people feel unwelcomed and constrained in the local church. Some find ways to be relevant by having their foot in the church while also having their hands and feet in other places—with people who may or may not be Christians. This generation needs leaders who have the capacity to think outside the box. Many young hip-hop prophets and activists protesting in the street are also the called-out ones, whom we can learn from and partner with. Doing so will require Christians to move beyond the racial, cultural, and social categories that have created a secular versus sacred binary. These rigid boundaries are often used to help people of faith feel safe and in control, but God is not limited by our finite boundaries. The Spirit is inviting people from every tribe, nation, culture, and ethnicity around the world to bring their true selves to the new understanding of church.

Why Center Race?

Reconciliation is a journey, a story. In my book *Roadmap to Reconciliation 2.0*, I define it as "an ongoing spiritual process, involving forgiveness, repentance and justice, that transforms broken relationships and systems to reflect God's original intention for all Creation to flourish."[1] To live into this definition, people must be rooted in a place or context. There is no such thing as generic, ready-made reconciliation. It demands contextual analysis and answers. It is not an abstract approach that never deals with anything substantive. My work is rooted in the places where I live, teach, and worship.

My work is also focused on the vexing issue of race, which is an especially potent and foundational evil in our country and around the world. The notion of race began with our Western philosophical heritage being shaped by ancient Greek thought. Greek philosophers such as Plato and Aristotle focused on categorization and differentiation, based on the belief that all reality was part of a "great chain of being." This logic suggests that there must be an ideal by which all others are compared. As time went on, this ideal led to a distorted anthropology that categorized people on a hierarchy of human difference, with some individuals closer to the ideal form of God and others further away. Plato's theory of forms also provided a philosophical rationale, known as dualism, that upheld the idea of a separation between the spirit and the body. This theory posited that the physical world was not as real or true as ideas, which led to a dichotomized worldview that saw the body, mind, and spirit as individual entities. This view is contrary to the biblical view of the self that understands humans to be holistic beings whose body, soul, and spirit are interconnected. Plato's notion that ideal reality is perfectly uniform, and therefore difference is inherently bad, produced a belief system that saw everything in the universe as ranked from lowest to highest perfection, from rocks to angels, based on how close it was to the pure form.

Armed with this philosophical belief system, Europeans began to explore the world. They encountered people who lived close to the land, honored the sacredness of animals, and connected with the Creator in the environment; they viewed such people as barbaric and primitive. Europeans perceived themselves to be civilized by comparison, which led them to believe that African, Asian, East Indian, West Indian, Aboriginal, South American, Indigenous, and Native American people were akin to animals and, therefore, lower on the human hierarchy. Europeans believed themselves to be more like God. Race permeated this belief during the Enlightenment period, naming Africans as "savages" and inferior, "Orientals" as second highest, and Europeans at the top. They created a social order based on a racialized system that affirmed their perceived superiority in comparison to other human beings.

We are now living with the consequences of that racialized philosophical worldview. Every aspect of our Western culture and modern society is anchored in this racial hierarchy of human difference. In our world, race profoundly determines where we live and our access to education, affordable health care, employment opportunities, professional networks, legal representation, financial security, environmental justice, healthy food options, social systems, and relationships—you name it. Even though science has proven race to be a social construct and not a biological reality, nothing in our society is unaffected by the man-made concept of race. It is still wreaking havoc on every aspect of our lives.

I center my work on addressing the evil of systemic racism, although I am also concerned about many other issues. As a woman, I know and have experienced the harm of gender discrimination and inequity. For most of my life, I felt that I had to choose one or the other, my race or my gender, when struggling to understand the mistreatment or discrimination

I was enduring. It never felt right, but somehow I felt like I had to rank which form of my marginalization mattered most. It wasn't until later that I internalized the intersectional nature of race. In November 2019, I was on a Ruby Woo pilgrimage led by Christian activist Lisa Sharon Harper. While traveling to one of our destinations, we watched a video clip of a 1978 American television miniseries entitled *A Woman Called Moses*, starring Cicely Tyson and based on the life of Harriet Tubman.

Tubman's master is portrayed as a man who admires her initiative and allows her to work a plot of land and keep the harvest profits. But he shows his true character when he learns that she has saved enough money to buy her freedom. He goes to her cabin on Sunday morning while she is getting dressed for church. He walks in and asks, "Ain't we fancy today?" She replies, "Just goin' to church, massa." He says he needs her to take a wagonload of goods into town. She is forlorn and her face immediately shows it. She turns to change out of her only Sunday dress when he says, "No, no. All you need to do is sit up on the wagon . . . and you'll be there in no time." He leaves and heads back to an elaborate party he is hosting on the lawn of his spacious mansion. Men and women are eating, dancing, and making merry while an old African enslaved man plays music on his fiddle. The women are dressed in beautiful antebellum dresses. When Harriet arrives, she goes directly to the wagon, but there is no mule hitched up to it. She looks perplexed when the slave owner comes down from the party to meet her. She says, "Where's the mule, massa?" He picks up the harness and hands it to her. Shock and fear immediately show on her face. She says, "Oh no, Massa! I can't pull this wagon by myself!" He snaps, "Sure you can, gal," and forces her to put on the harness and drag the loaded wagon to the point of collapse, causing her Sunday dress to rip off her body in pieces.

What was most horrifying for me was seeing the white women laughing and jeering as they see another woman being humiliated in front of them. In that moment I saw the power of racism. It was more advantageous for those women to be white than to identify with being female. One of the chief functions of race is to distance white people from those of a different race.

This country and many others have centuries of history of destroying Black and Brown bodies based on such racist ideology. The weight of living in a Brown, Black, yellow, differently abled, or queer body still means life-or-death struggle for far too many people. Health care is revoked for some folks due to their appearance, sexual orientation, citizenship, gender, or socioeconomic status. Safety is never guaranteed to bodies that those in power perceive as lesser, weaker, or undeserving. It is into this world of brokenness and division that we are called to be agents of reconciliation. As Christians we are to engage with others in ways that lead to healing and change in the world around us. This work was initiated by God, and we are invited into the spiritual process of making all things new as we work together with others. This must involve actively addressing the intersectional impact of racism that is destroying our country, our communities, and the people we love.

The Soul of Nehemiah

I believe the book of Nehemiah can help us explore a new way to achieve this vision. Before proceeding, though, I must first acknowledge that many scholars question Nehemiah's historical accuracy. For example, it seems unlikely for the building of Jerusalem to have made considerable progress during the reign of King Artaxerxes. Further, Nehemiah is told that the city is still in ruins, which reveals that the timeline might be off in Nehemiah's account based on the material that can be traced to various sources. Admittedly, there are some discrepancies in the exact timing of circumstances and events throughout this book. But regardless, this is still the Word of God, and I believe Nehemiah holds truth that is informative for our lives.

But even more disturbing to me was the concern I received from a dear white brother, who asked me to reconsider Ezra-Nehemiah through a postcolonial lens. He argued that these biblical texts have been weaponized by Christians to support the exclusion of others. A poignant example of this occurred on January 20, 2017, at a private pre-inauguration religious service for Donald Trump. The speaker for this event was Rev. Robert Jeffress, a Southern Baptist pastor, who referenced the book of Nehemiah in his message:

> When I think of you, President-elect Trump, I am reminded of another great leader God chose thousands of years ago in Israel. The nation had been in bondage for decades, the infrastructure of the country was in shambles, and God raised up a powerful leader to restore the nation. And the man God chose was neither a politician nor a priest. Instead, God chose a builder whose name was Nehemiah. And the first step of rebuilding the nation was the building of a great wall. God instructed Nehemiah to build a wall around Jerusalem to protect its citizens from enemy attack. You see, God is NOT against building walls![2]

Jeffress's interpretation of the Bible's wall-building stories, espoused by many evangelical Christians in the United

States, suggests that the divine intent behind the book of Nehemiah is abundantly clear: God is the builder (and rebuilder) of walls. In this way of thinking, God condones the divisive practice of building walls to keep out people who are immigrants, refugees, and foreigners! This is not the God I know. This concern caused me to struggle to find a clear sense of direction while writing this book. When I write, I typically have a clear idea of my purpose, and God guides me along the way. But this time was different. I had lost my point of view and was looking at Nehemiah through a lens that was not authentic. As I listened to the concerns of my well-meaning white brother, I had failed to take my own identity into account. His postcolonial interpretation that wanted to reject Nehemiah as exclusionary differed from my interpretation that found Nehemiah to be focused on rebuilding the people, and I was feeling conflicted by these varying interpretations. During this time, I confided in one of my colleagues about feeling stuck. He reminded me that it was valid and appropriate for me to read Nehemiah through the lens of my own—Black—experience and perspective. His words were the consolation I needed.

You would think I—a professor, preacher, and author on racial reconciliation—would naturally be rooted in my identity and always operate from this psychological and spiritual perspective. Yet, time and time again, I'm reminded of how whiteness has embedded itself into the academy, including biblical scholarship. I've decided to authentically share my perspective and be anchored in my own self and social location. I agree that Nehemiah and many other biblical books have been used by those in power to keep people out rather than to let the good news invite all people in. However, I believe Nehemiah also speaks to and from the perspective of those who have been kidnapped, trafficked, and enslaved for four hundred years. Through Nehemiah, God is saying, "I'm going to rebuild you a place of safety and dignity where you can prosper and will not be destroyed."

This message is especially pertinent to people who are marginalized or have experienced the horror of racial violence. Consider the example of the affluent African American community of the Greenwood District in Tulsa, Oklahoma, after World War I. This was a thriving business district and residential area known as Black Wall Street. Tragically, on May 31 and June 1, 1921, in response to a young Black man being arrested for a white woman's accusation, public officials armed and deputized a mob of white men, who demolished the Greenwood District. They stole and destroyed personal property left behind in homes and businesses of the Black people who fled for their lives. These vigilantes, some of whom were government agents, deliberately burned or otherwise destroyed an estimated 1,256 homes, along with other structures—including churches, schools, businesses, even a hospital and a library. In the wake of this violence, thirty-five city blocks lay in charred ruins, more than eight hundred people were treated for injuries, and historians believe that as many as three hundred people were killed. This act of terrorism, destruction of property, and loss of life is referred to as the Tulsa Race Massacre.

Now, imagine if those Black people were asked by the white men who committed these unthinkable acts of brutality to join their oppressors in rebuilding the Greenwood District. How do you think they might feel and respond? I would assume they would unequivocally say no, which would be completely understandable. I ultimately rejected that decolonizing way of reading the Scriptures because it felt like the oppressor telling the oppressed how to rebuild. I needed to reclaim the text. My perspective on decoloniz- ing the Scriptures is rooted in the recognition that the Bible is read and interpreted differently when it is read from the bottom up rather than the top down. Decolonizing the Scrip- tures seeks and needs interpretations from readers who have been marginalized by white, European, Christian, male, het- eronormative supremacy.

After grappling with the complexities in Nehemiah, I'm still compelled by the implicit promise of restoration and revitalization in this narrative. I believe this book helps us explore practical ways to bring restoration to our communi- ties. The soul of Nehemiah offers not a political worldview but a biblical one that directly points to what God cares about. Nehemiah sees the ethnic, social, and political divide between the Jews and the Persians. He is concerned with rebuilding the city of God—the place where his people once found their protection and identity. Although he was born in exile, he rose to the position of cupbearer to the Persian king. This key role provided him with confidential access to power. He was trusted. Like many of us who go away to college or attain financial success, Nehemiah lived at ease with some degree of privilege. He did not, however, forget his identity as an Israelite who cared deeply about his people, who were in a dehumanizing state of distress. He used his proximity to the king to influence those in power and mobilize his people to repair the brokenness around them.

A Revitalizing Movement

Like Nehemiah, we are also called to identify with and care about those in troubling situations. Such people in disturbing circumstances can be found not only outside the church but also in Christian churches, institutions, and organizations. Faith communities are being torn apart by the political and cultural wars in society. This increased sense of hostility and polarization has led to declining church attendance and lower enrollment in Christian colleges and seminaries. These vehement disagreements over wedge issues like abortion, sexuality, multiculturalism, racism, guns, and other cultural conflicts are destroying our witness and credibility as Christians.

It is amid these difficult challenges that Nehemiah gives us a model for revitalizing our communities. As followers of Jesus, we have been entrusted with the work of reconciliation that repairs broken relationships, systems, and structures. We do this in partnership with others to embody God's love, justice, and healing in the world. I have hope that this is possible because I see the flame of God working in this next generation to ignite a revitalizing movement. I observe their concern for those on the margins. I see them searching for ways to address racial inequity and social injustice. I also hear them asking for seasoned guidance as they navigate a new way forward.

I've chosen to anchor my prophetic call to these emerging leaders in the action-oriented biblical narrative of Nehemiah. I'm not trying to defend Nehemiah, and I'm not saying that everything he did was right. However, I am convinced that he tried to do something to make a difference. I see similarities in how this generation desperately wants to see change. Like Nehemiah, they enter this work knowing they may not always succeed and there will be times when they fail. That's okay because their actions will demonstrate that they are sincerely trying to address the unjust systems and structures that prevent all people from thriving.

Since you're reading this book, I believe you want to be part of this movement of God. I see you and want to inspire and empower you to do that. As a professor of reconciliation studies and a pastor at a multiracial, multicultural, intergenerational church, I have watched a young generation of Christians and listened intently to the Holy Spirit on their behalf. That's why I believe I have a word for the next generation and for all followers of Jesus. My years of experience at the lectern of Christian academic institutions and in the pulpit of Christian churches, along with my proximity to especially the next generation's passion for justice, has afforded me a unique lens to see both the past mistakes and the future promise that intersect in the present. I hope you will actively apply the practical principles throughout this book in your various spheres of influence—business, the arts, music, technology, ministry, childcare, education, sports, journalism, medicine, social work, communications, and so on—because reconciliation is needed everywhere in our hurting world. I also hope that you will come to believe that revitalization is possible: the next generation offers great hope, and every major spiritual movement around the world started among young people. This movement, rooted in the story of Nehemiah, can start with you.

ONE

Ask the Right Questions

These are the words of Nehemiah, Hacaliah's son. In the month of Kislev, in the twentieth year, while I was in the fortress city of Susa, Hanani, one of my brothers, came with some other men from Judah. I asked them about the Jews who had escaped and survived the captivity, and about Jerusalem. They told me, "Those in the province who survived the captivity are in great trouble and shame! The wall around Jerusalem is broken down, and its gates have been destroyed by fire!"

—Nehemiah 1:1-3

I became convinced of the importance of asking questions through a chance encounter with a fellow student at Fuller Theological Seminary. I was worried about something that seemed monumental at the time, and the anxiety was obvious on my face. As I walked across campus, I saw another

African American seminarian, Roland Wallace, walking toward me. When we reached each other, he immediately asked, "What's going on with you? What's wrong?" I poured out my heart and shared my tale of woes, and then he said, "Brenda, the wrong question will always lead to the wrong answer. It's more important to ask yourself, Am I asking the right question?" Although I can't remember what it was that had upset me, I will never forget the profound truth of what Roland said that day.

The value of questioning is also supported by studies of healthy human development. Irving Sigel, a pioneer and leader in the study of children's intellectual development, devoted his life to understanding the significance of asking questions. He believed that the brain responds to questions in ways that promote social, emotional, and cognitive development. Asking questions fosters an alternative and complex representation of stories, events, and circumstances. It also fosters a more wide-ranging ability to process the world, which is a distinct advantage to learning. In short, questions create challenges that make us learn.

A learner is by nature a questioner. If there is a desire in a person to increase their knowledge, skills, or understanding, it's driven by doubt, curiosity, wonderment, uncertainty, and recognition of a need. This drive is focused through questions that the learner formulates and actively seeks to answer. They may be simple questions that seek clear facts, or complex questions that probe deep into concepts, beliefs, and understandings. But however simple or complex an issue, a good, clear, and relevant question—the right question—will be more useful to the learner than a question that is vague, poorly defined, or irrelevant. Thinking is central to all learning, and it is our questions that fuel and drive our thinking.

I have personally come to believe and have experienced this to be profoundly true in my own life. It started when I became a Christian as a nineteen-year-old sophomore at Rutgers University. As a result of my conversion, I went to a Campus Crusade meeting with a friend, another Black student who grew up in a conservative Bible church in upstate New York. When we walked into the small auditorium, I noticed that my friend and I were the only Black students in the room. Even though no one told me I was unwelcome, I felt the foreignness. Almost ten years later, as a third-year seminary student, I began my practicum as the chaplain's assistant at Occidental College. In this role, I was given the freedom to choose the area of ministry I wanted to pursue. As a woman in ministry, I assumed I would devote my time to mentoring Christian female leaders. However, when I walked into the weekly chapel service for the first time, I was stunned to see two hundred students in attendance. At the time, Occidental had 1,200 undergraduates in their student body, so to have two hundred people in chapel was a significant number. As I looked around the modern and beautifully designed chapel, I was also surprised to see that there were only two students of color in the crowd—a Latino male student and a young African American man. It felt like a time warp from the days when I was a college student at Rutgers years earlier. Nothing had changed regarding race!

As I stood there perplexed, a question rose from deep inside me: What is it about the issue of race that is so difficult for Christians to make any real progress on addressing? Little did I know, but that question would lead me to focus on racial reconciliation as my life's work.

Many years later, I now work with reconciliation leaders to help them identify their most pressing questions. I encourage them to bring the real concerns they are currently facing. We then work together to clarify their most pressing question. This is usually a question that they have continually wrestled with for a long time. Often, it is a question they've never consciously articulated, but it is a concern they see. Some example questions include: What does it mean to be rooted in our community of origin, but also move out and still carry the concerns and cares of that community with us? What does it mean to embody that community in whatever space we find ourselves? How do we stay connected while being disconnected by the realities of socioeconomic, educational, and geographical distance? We may never fully answer our burning questions, but they will serve as beacons in the distance that point us in the direction of our life's work.

Starting with a Question

It is easy to feel uncertain about where to begin. Nehemiah started with a pressing question about the suffering of the people he cared about. He identified with them and wanted to hear how they were doing. Nehemiah questioned his brother, Hanani, and the group of men with him, who had come to Susa from Judah.

Susa, one of several Persian capitals, was located about one hundred miles north of the Persian Gulf. It was an influential center with religious importance that also became a commercial, administrative, and political hub. Susa enjoyed many different cultural influences because of its strategic position along ancient trade routes. As a verb, Susa means "to take away or to remove," which is interesting because Nehemiah was born to Jewish parents in Persia during their exile from Jerusalem.

The city of Jerusalem was completely conquered by the Babylonians, and the once-glorious temple of Solomon was destroyed. When the Babylonians conquered Jerusalem, they deported the top tier of society: nobility, clergy, officials, learned people, scribes, and so on. The government was completely removed from the city and the region. For almost seventy years Jerusalem was something of a ghost town, with the potential to end up like many ancient cities—forgotten except to history. During Nehemiah's time, the Persian Empire reached its greatest extent, engulfing nearly the entire Near East. The Persians, under Cyrus the Great, defeated the Babylonians and absorbed the lands of Israel and Judah into their empire. The next year, Cyrus allowed the people of Judah, now called Jews, to return home and rebuild the temple of the Lord.

In the meantime, Nehemiah, living far away from home, had acquired a level of influence and position. He lived in the fortified palace of the Persians as cupbearer to King Artaxerxes I. Although his body was in Persia, Nehemiah's heart was back home in Jerusalem. He identified with his compatriots despite his social status and great privilege. He asked how the people and the city he loved were doing. Nehemiah asked the right question.

The response he got was not good. He learned that the walls had been destroyed and the gates had been ruined by fire. The city and its people were therefore vulnerable.

I wonder what the response would be if someone asked a similar question today: How is America doing? How are its most vulnerable populations? The response, I fear, would be as devastating as the news Nehemiah received. For example, at the time of this writing in April 2023, there had been 190 mass shootings in the United States in 2023, thirteen of them occurring in a school.[1] A mass shooting is defined by the Gun Violence Archive as an incident in which four or more victims are shot, either killed or injured.[2] In an incident in Nashville, three children and three staff members were shot and killed at the Covenant School, a Christian school for students in preschool through sixth grade. In Michigan, three students were killed and five others were injured when a gunman opened fire at two locations on Michigan State University's campus in East Lansing. In another incident of random violence, California saw three shootings in a matter of days, with one shooting leaving eleven people dead and nine others injured after a gunman opened fire at a dance studio near a Lunar New Year celebration.

Generations Z and Alpha are sick and tired of having their lives put on the line because of other people's inability or unwillingness to effect change. Even the very people fighting for change are being punished for pushing against the status quo. For example, in response to the Covenant School shooting in Tennessee, seven thousand students and educators went to the State Capitol and demanded that the general assembly take action to protect them against the real threat of guns. In an act of solidarity and empathy, they were visibly supported by three Democratic representatives. In retaliation, the Tennessee House of Representatives—comprised of a primarily white, conservative majority—voted to expel Representatives Justin Jones and Justin Pearson, both Black men, for leading a protest in support of these students. The third protestor, a white woman, was not expelled. Expulsion has generally been reserved as a punishment for lawmakers accused of serious misconduct, not as a weapon against political opponents. These legislators preferred to punish those who stood with the protestors instead of taking courageous action to enact gun control legislation. When asked why she was not expelled for the protest but her colleagues were, Rep. Gloria Johnson said it was because she is white and they are Black.

It is heartbreaking to think of the social calamity we're facing right now. Climate change and inept responses to it have left our environment in ruins; children's ability to trust parents, pastors, priests, and politicians has been destroyed; the credibility of the church is in shambles; commitment to truth and academic excellence is in question; books are being banned from schools; and children are forbidden to learn about our racial history in America. In addition, our political systems, voting rights, and our medical, educational, and technological superiority are diminished; even our integrity as a global example of democracy, civility, liberty, and justice is almost destroyed.

Add to that a global pandemic, cyberattacks, environmental disasters, and mass shootings, and we might reasonably fear these are apocalyptic signs of the end times. This is the world in which the next generation of Christian leaders must discern the truth as people called to reconciliation. These leaders are faced with daunting challenges because, like the rest of us, they have never experienced anything like this before. As a result, they are full of questions and painfully unsure about how the future will unfold.

I am reminded of a conversation I had with the first few students graduating with a reconciliation studies degree from Seattle Pacific University. As a new professor hired to teach and direct the program, I was deeply troubled to hear one young woman say that she was afraid to tell people she had minored in reconciliation studies. She was afraid that others would expect her to demonstrate her knowledge and skills as a reconciler, but she was unsure she could do it. I felt like we had failed this student, because in my perception, her doubt reflected a lack of preparedness. After all, these students had invested time and resources to learn how to be reconcilers. I thought they should emerge from their dedicated field of study fully confident, equipped, and ready to go.

But now I know that uncertainty is part of reconciliation. To do this work, we must be willing to grapple with complexity and ask ourselves, Do we care enough to weep about the state of inequality, inequity, and injustice in our country and around the world? Are we close enough to listen to and learn from people who may look, live, and believe differently than we do? Often, as leaders, we believe we must have all the answers, but the truth is that we need to ask more questions. We live in a world that suggests we should know, but we could be more effective if we start to ask the right questions.

Asking questions is not always easy when you are used to being the source of the solution. Our ability to ask questions requires humility—to admit how much we don't know. This humility enables the deeper exploration required for us to move from vague surface sentiments to the core issue. It is not good enough to feel bad about a social issue or to send thoughts and prayers. We must dig deeper, searching our own souls with an unrelenting gaze to discover a way that will lead to tangible action. Our most pressing question should compel and motivate us to get involved.

Our questions can also help us develop empathy toward those who are suffering and inform how we can get actively involved. It is in this search for answers that we can discover new, creative methods of innovation and change. Neil Postman, an author, educator, media theorist, and cultural critic, explains, "All our knowledge results from questions, which is another way of saying that questioning is our most important intellectual tool."[3] I'm convinced that Christian leaders must learn to be comfortable with the discomfort of not knowing and must endeavor to ask the most burning questions of this generation to be effective. When we strive to do this, it leads to solidarity with the people we seek to love and serve.

Listening to Others' Stories

After hearing the answer to his pressing question, Nehemiah is distraught by the news that the people and city he loves are in a state of crisis: "The wall around Jerusalem is broken down, and its gates have been destroyed by fire!" (1:3). He sees himself as part of these people and identifies with their suffering. Nehemiah knows what this disaster means, because in ancient times, a city wall was an important defense. The wall would be strong and tall and the top would be flat so that the guards could walk on the surface. From that position, they could watch for any criminals inside the city. The guards would also be able to see an enemy army approaching. The wall had large gates that were kept open during the day. Traders and travelers could enter the city, and the people could go to the market. By night, the guards closed the gates so that nobody could enter, and the city would be safe. With the wall of Jerusalem broken and the gates destroyed, the condition of the inhabitants was precarious, as they could become easy victims. Nehemiah was deeply concerned for them.

Like Nehemiah, when we interrogate ourselves and the world around us, we become aware of the complexity people are facing, which leads to empathy and true compassion. We realize that our lives and our cultures are composed of many overlapping stories. Hearing these stories helps us practice empathetic listening and communication skills because they challenge us to wrestle with the complex realities of life. When we engage with stories, we are given the opportunity to enter into other people's lives and perspectives, and it encourages us to value and to share our own unique story. It's important not just to question others but also to be open to questioning ourselves. Self-inquiry helps us tell the truth in our own stories. As we do this, we can develop new eyes to see, decode, and understand what is happening in the world around us.

How do you listen to other people's stories? How do you understand your own? Stories can help us change our core values. Through stories we can expand our partial understanding of ourselves, others, the world, and even God. Neurologists have discovered that our brains seem to be wired for stories. When we hear or experience stories, especially while listening to music, it's like a type of virtual reality that causes neurotransmitters in the brain to have a spike in dopamine, producing a physiological reaction that moves us toward willful suspension of disbelief.[4] Listening to others talk about their problems or emotions that we also feel can give us a sense that they know what we're going through, which can help us navigate tough times.

Wes Moore, an investment banker, author, television producer, nonprofit executive, and the first Black governor of Maryland, reflects on the power of stories, especially stories told through music:

Hip-hop had begun to play a special role in my life. It wasn't just music and lyrics. It was a validator. In my struggle to reconcile my two worlds, it was an essential asset. By the late 1980s, hip-hop had graduated from being the underground art of the Bronx to a rising global culture. My obsession with hip-hop kept me credible with the kids in my neighborhood. It let them know that, regardless of my school affiliation, I still understood. . . . But even more than that, I found in hip-hop, the sound of my generation talking to itself, working through the fears and anxieties and inchoate dreams—of wealth or power or revolution or success—we all shared.[5]

There are always stories within stories and a worldview that underpins the story being told. It's essential to recognize that everyone's life is a story. However, we can't tell our story if we don't know it. Many people have not learned to listen to their own story or to the stories of others. Worse yet, there are those who try to destroy the narratives that sustain people's identities and substitute it with narratives of their own.

In his book *Reconciliation: Mission and Ministry in a Changing Social Order*, Robert J. Schreiter calls these "narratives of the lie." These distorted stories are intended to negate the truth of a people's own narratives and are ultimately an act of violence. Schreiter explains:

> What is at issue here is the fact that we humans cannot survive without a narrative of identity. Without some narrative, we slide into chaos that is death for animals without instincts. That is why narratives—any narratives—are better than no narratives at all. The purpose of torture, imprisonment, and coercion is not to end narratives—that is done most efficiently by execution—but to provide another narrative so that people will learn to live with and acquiesce to the will of the oppressor.[6]

As reconcilers, our job is to redeem the narrative. Schreiter adds, "It is only when we discover and embrace a redeeming narrative that we can be liberated from the lie's seductive and cunning power."[7] This kind of liberating and healing work was the goal of the Truth and Reconciliation Commission in

South Africa. This courtlike body was created to investigate gross human rights violations perpetrated during the period of apartheid. These horrible acts of violence included abductions, killings, and torture. As he recalled the power of the numerous stories he heard, Archbishop Desmond Tutu said, "We found that many who came to the commission attested afterward to the fact that they had found relief and experienced healing, just through the process of telling their story. The acceptance, the affirmation, the acknowledgement that they had indeed suffered was cathartic for them."[8]

Christianity offers a larger narrative to which we can connect our own stories, and it offers a memory that can serve as a framework to rebuild our shattered story. A dear friend and colleague, internationally recognized scholar Willie James Jennings, once said that if he could be anything in society, he would want to be the storyteller. When I asked why, he said that the storytellers determine the narrative. Stories take us beyond theory and move us to engage with real people. Stories provide a more complete picture of the statistics being cited, the facts being debated, and the superficial understandings of the problems we face.

Nigerian writer Chimamanda Adichie insightfully warns us to beware of what she calls "the danger of a single story." When we listen to only one story about a people or nation, we ignore the complex reality of their experiences. She encourages people to understand that "when we reject the single story, when we realize there is never a single story about any place, we regain a kind of paradise."[9]

What is your story?' What characters populate your story? How have you seen God writing reconciliation into your life story? I believe that all of us are born with purpose written into our DNA and that God is ultimately the author of our stories. Like Nehemiah, we are living in a time when the sociopolitical structures we have built are not working. We are past the point of simply reforming or rebuilding—we must create something new. Crisis points can often lead to change. Reconciliation is rooted in the recognition that we're in trouble.

As you wrestle with the complexities of life, pay attention to what sparks a burning question in you and ignites a fire in you to get involved. These questions that come from within us are the origins of stories that we did not realize we had the capacity to tell or explore. They are the fuel that prompts us to interrogate the stories of the places we inhabit, the people we know, and the institutions we attend. Questions lead us to find answers, and the pursuit of answers leads us deeper into our stories and the stories of the world around us. I've found that as you do this, God will fan the flame and write a new chapter in the narrative of your life that puts you on a path toward your purpose and a story worth living.

TWO

Identify with the Plight of People

When I heard this news, I sat down and wept. I mourned for days, fasting and praying before the God of heaven. I said: "LORD God of heaven, great and awesome God, you are the one who keeps covenant and is truly faithful to those who love you and keep your commandments. Let your ear be attentive and your eyes open to hear the prayer of your servant, which I now pray before you night and day for your servants, the people of Israel."

—Nehemiah 1:4–6

Sometimes the answers to our questions will break our hearts. Nehemiah would know.

Nehemiah was devastated when he heard that "those in the province who survived the captivity are in great trouble and shame!" (1:3). This powerful man broke down and wept.

Although he was geographically removed from the destruction of his people, he remained proximate to their plight.

What we see in Nehemiah's response is lament. A lament is a cry for help in times of trouble or suffering. When I visited Israel-Palestine in 2017, I experienced what it truly felt like to lament. I was at the Western Wall, also known as the Wailing Wall. It is a portion of an ancient limestone wall that connects to the hill known as the Temple Mount. This wall is referred to as the Wailing Wall because of the Jewish practice of coming to the site to mourn and bemoan the destruction of the temple. When I approached this wall, which is separated into sections for men and women, I found myself in a crowd of women who were pressing to get closer to the wall as they poured out their hearts to God. I was reminded of the verse in Jeremiah in which God calls the wailing women forward. I decided I wanted to get close enough to the wall to touch it, to create a sacred space for myself to lament.

To my surprise, as I thought about the state of affairs in the United States and in my personal life, especially my concern for the future of my children in a country that was becoming increasingly unsafe for them under the Trump administration, I started praying out loud with words that eventually became tears. I was so focused on pouring out my personal petitions that everything else became blocked out, and my sole focus was on God. I did not know who was next to me, and it didn't matter. The only thing that mattered was the personal connection between me and God. I recognized my own loss of control, and I understood that I could not fix any of this on my own. That was difficult for me, as someone who is used to being able to work hard and get things done. Letting go of all that at the Wailing Wall was like recognizing the limits of my humanity. But I also felt that

I had God's full and undivided attention. God was listening to my wails. I felt that the Lord was there to carry my burden so that when I left I was not holding on to it anymore.

Lament takes wordless, almost unbearable pain and gives it a shape and a voice. Lament provides a language to vocalize, empathize, and memorialize any kind of pain, but especially the pain that stems from racial injustice. In the Black cultural tradition, lamentation most often appears in music, from spirituals to gospel hymns to the blues. In music we can name the reality of life and find comfort in expressing it in a community of others who can relate. Nowhere is this more true than in the Black church. The Black church understands the importance of lament to give people hope, resilience, and strength.

Another way to think about lament is that it is a form of truth-telling. It means being honest about our own sin and failures, if it is a lament of repentance. Or it means truthfully naming sinful structures or injustices that harm us or others, if it is a lament of protest. Cole Arthur Riley, author of *This Here Flesh*, puts it this way: "I don't know if I've encountered better emotional truth-telling than when visiting Black churches."[1]

Given the experience of Black people in this country over many generations, it is no accident that lament is so deeply rooted in the Black church. The persistent presence of oppression born from the transatlantic slave trade, perfected through Jim Crow and manifested in nearly every system created by this country, results in an environment ripe for lament. Lament was born on the bottom of the slave ship and the auction block. It was sung in the cotton and rice fields and quietly whispered under the overseers' lash.

In addition to the extreme physical demands and horrific treatment that brutalized and dehumanized enslaved African people, they also faced enormous obstacles to practicing their faith. The plantation owners often refused to allow the human beings they enslaved to gather for worship because they feared that the truth of God's Word would embolden them to seek freedom. That's why enslaved Black people met secretly in "hush harbors," covert worship services in the woods or swamps. In these sacred, secret gathering places, songs of lament provided refuge.

The spirituals expressed emotions for both the individual and the entire community. They also provided suffering people with a personalized voice to strengthen their faith. These songs offered a safe space for suffering and provided a language of hope for those who lived in exile. Every spiritual expressed a unique perspective on the overwhelming hardship of slavery and segregation. Songs like "Swing Low, Sweet Chariot" offered hope for a better tomorrow while songs like "Sometimes I Feel Like a Motherless Child" captured feelings of abandonment, loneliness, and a desperate need for God's help. In his book *The Color of Compromise*, Jemar Tisby writes,

> The Negro spiritual put black lamentations into songs that soared upward as prayers for God to save them and grant them the perseverance to exist and resist. Through their understanding of Scripture, black Christians sang, "His eye is on the sparrow, and I know he watches me." They looked to the book of Exodus and saw God saving the Israelites from slavery. In the white slaveowners they saw "old Pharaoh" and knew they could pray, "Let my people go."[2]

The Black church was born from this legacy of people who cried out to God with passion, faith, and exuberance. People formed by this tradition know that lament means talking to God about what is wrong in the world. It is and continues to be a crucial spiritual practice for the Black church because it is the biblical language for both our pain and our protest. It was the spiritual songs of the Black church that played a unifying and galvanizing role in the civil rights movement. Many familiar songs, such as "We Shall Overcome," have their roots in this rich tradition, and they have empowered people to keep marching and fighting for justice and human rights. The communal lament cemented by these hymns moved people toward one another rather than pushing them apart.

The power of lament to connect people through communal compassion is the reason the work of reconciliation must be connected to the suffering of the people we care about. Nehemiah heard heartbreaking news and was so affected by that news that he cried out to God as if the events were happening to him. The same should be true of us. Hearing reports of human suffering should cause God's people to weep regardless of how physically or experientially distant we may be from the pain. Nehemiah's lament embodies his empathy for his people. Although he did nothing wrong, he confessed the sin of his people and identified with them. He admitted his complicity in the problem and saw himself in the people. The renowned priest, professor, writer, and theologian Henri Nouwen says that this must be the posture of a leader:

> For all ministers are called to recognize the sufferings of their time in their own hearts, and to make that recognition the starting point of their service. Whether we try to enter into a dislocated world, relate to a convulsive generation, or

speak to a dying person, our service will not be perceived as authentic unless it comes from a heart wounded by the suffering about which we speak. Thus, nothing can be written about ministry without a deeper understanding of the ways in which ministers can make their own wounds available as a source of healing.[3]

Leaders must be proximate to their constituency. They must be close enough to let the gravity of people's suffering touch them. The great philosopher, theologian, and civil rights leader Howard Thurman often said that every great leader's story is rooted in care and concern for "people whose backs are up against the wall."[4]

Those who seek to do this work must ask themselves, Do we care enough to weep about the state of racial and social injustice in our world? If so, Robert Schreiter offers the next step: "We begin by acknowledging the violence that is being done to us, and we cry out in protest and lament against it. Silence is the friend of oppression."[5] This cry of protest is what happened in the civil rights movement through the tradition of lament in the Black church. It is what must happen now.

Overcoming Our Silence

Recovering the biblical practice of lament can help the church speak where it is tempted toward silence. As people refuse to be silent, it is important to acknowledge that the land and locations where we live are also crying out. In the Hebrew Bible, mourning is an expansive practice that includes the land. To take the land's mourning seriously is to ask about its grief—to wonder what truth the land is telling us. To help us explore this question, Andi Lloyd calls us to consider our human connection to the land:

> The land's lament speaks a foundational ecological truth: when one part of creation goes awry, the whole suffers. The land's grief at what the people have done points to the fundamental reality of our interconnection. Perhaps it is the boundedness of our bodies that makes it so easy to overlook the truth of our connectedness. We appear so discrete, so unitary, but we are not.[6]

It is difficult, if not impossible, to separate the plight of people from where they live. My colleague David Leong, in an article entitled "The Theology of a Collapsed Condo Building," examines what really caused the partial collapse of a twelve-story beachfront condominium in a suburb of Miami, Florida. It became clear that this tragedy wasn't just a random incident; it resulted from a shaky foundation. He writes:

> The terrible collapse was not only a failure of physical structures—steel and concrete eroded by natural elements and neglect—but it was also a failure of social structures due to organizational infighting, institutional gridlock, and urban wealth disparities. . . .
>
> For too long, the Christian imagination has divorced our identities and social worlds from geography, as if we exist in the abstract, apart from the land and the built environment we inhabit. But what if who we are—and especially who we are together—is completely dependent on the everyday spaces we inhabit, like high-rise condos and retirement communities?[7]

This tragic example demonstrates how the fabric that connects all of creation is badly torn by injustice, exploitative systems, and ideologies of scarcity that promote a zero-sum-game mentality. Therefore, to lament is to speak truth to the lies that prop up the status quo. In mourning together in true solidarity, we collectively bear witness to what is wrong. The pandemic cast a bright light on the numerous systemic injustices and the ways the church has turned a blind eye to those inequities. As the number of Covid-related deaths rose and news outlets showed video after video of unarmed Black people dying at the hands of police or vigilantes, many Christians discovered that they had never been given the necessary tools to lament.

During this frightening time, so many people, Christians included, felt powerless. The virus was raging, people were dying, and there was nothing people could do except stay home. Those deemed essential workers put themselves and their families at personal risk. Cities across America went dark. Businesses closed. Restaurants failed. People lost their jobs and their livelihoods. The isolation and the devastation forced many to confront and acknowledge their own limitations. There was literally nothing anyone could do. The entire matter was out of our hands. There was an overwhelming sense of helplessness everywhere. The "blessed assurance" many clung to previously in their Christian journey was not available amid such unprecedented calamity. Empty platitudes and trite expressions of faith were insufficient in the face of so much sickness, death, and inequity. It was in this moment that many realized that their Christian upbringings and formation had not prepared them for this level of uncertainty. They did not know how to lament.

The pandemic had a particularly harsh impact on young people. Sent home from school suddenly, with familiar rites of passage canceled and plans deferred, all of it impossible to restore. The sureness with which we had all indoctrinated American youth was stripped from them in a moment. Many of them, too young to recall Trayvon Martin and whose eyes may have been shielded from Eric Garner, were confronted repeatedly by George Floyd's cries for his own mother, a knee on his neck, his pleas ignored until life and breath were choked from him. Young people responded with action to the uncertainty surrounding them and the suffering so apparent as they scrolled through their social media feed. Their grief spilled onto the streets, their shouts filled the air, and their cries crashed through storefront windows. These young people could have benefited from hearing from Christians who could model lament.

Lament helps us recognize the pain of others and leads us to a deeper understanding of how we got here. Cole Arthur Riley explains why this is crucial to the credibility and witness of Christians:

I am most disillusioned with the Christian faith when in the presence of a Christian who refuses to name the traumas of this world. I am suspicious of anyone who can observe colonization, genocide, and decay in the world and not be stirred to lament in some way. For all the goodness of God, my ancestors were still abducted from their homes, raped, and enslaved. I will not be rushed out of my sorrow for it. And we can delight that God made the garden with all those trees of fruit to feast on, but the earth is ailing and eroding from overconsumption and neglect. I shouldn't need to recite a litany of wounds and injustices and decay in order to justify my sadness. In lament, our task is never to convince someone of the brokenness of this world; it is to convince them of the world's worth in the first place. True lament is not born from the trite sentiment that the

54

world is bad but rather from a deep conviction that it is worthy of goodness.[8]

Lament is a form of hope. It is a cry from our souls that says, "It doesn't have to be this way!" By mourning together in solidarity, we name the truth of what's wrong with the world and, in doing so, we are motivated to make it right. Andi Lloyd says that as the land mourns, it joins us in our deep desire for a better world. She writes,

> The land's mourning speaks simultaneously of a vision of the world as it ought to be—that beautiful fabric—and the truth of the world as it is: too much injustice and too little love fraying the threads that hold us all. The land feels those fraying threads. The land grieves those fraying threads. The land mourns.[9]

Our lament is prophetic speech. It bears faithful witness to the fact that all is not right with the world and, consequently, all is not right with us. We wouldn't be disappointed or saddened if we did not believe something better and more life-giving is possible. The practice of lament is our commitment to keeping hope alive. Riley explains:

> Lament is not anti-hope. It's not even a stepping-stone to hope. Lament itself *is* a form of hope. It's an innate awareness that what is should not be. As if something is written on our hearts that tells us exactly what we are meant for, and whenever confronted with something contrary to this, we experience a crumbling. And in the rubble, we say, *God, you promised*. We ask, *WHY*? And how could we experience such a devastation if we were not, on some mysterious plane, hoping for something different. Our hope can be only as deep as our lament is. And our lament as deep as our hope.[10]

When we lament, we align ourselves with the heart of God. There might be times that we seek to please or obey God, but lament changes that posture to one of acknowledging our need for God. It also introduces us to the care of God. Sometimes we need to experience God as a mother who hears her child crying in the middle of the night and rushes to where we are to comfort and console us—assuring us that we're going to be all right. This familiar narrative is found in the psalms of lament. These beautiful poems or hymns express our human struggles. In them, prayers are laid out before the Lord about troubling situations and requests are made for God's help and tender care.

Writing laments or liturgies of lament can be a spiritual practice to help people express their grief about the inequity and injustices plaguing our world today. In an interview about practicing lament, theologian and author Rebekah Eklund introduces tools to help people write their laments. She encourages people to write laments using a fourfold pattern that entails invocation, complaint, petition, and trust. An invocation includes calling on the name of someone who will listen, often God. Complaint is when you pour out your heart about the grievance that has happened. A petition is a request for something to be done to rectify the problem. And you close with a word of trust, believing that your petition will be heard and justice will be served. This fourfold pattern follows the same structure as the psalms of lament. Many average churchgoers and Bible readers are not terribly aware of how large a section of the psalms is lament. In fact, complaint and petition are the most common type of psalm. That is an indicator that we're not just allowed to lament, but we really should be lamenting. Eklund details how lament has influenced her own church context: "I used to be part of a church that held regular services of prayer for healing, and those services were naturally full of lament. I live in Baltimore now, and, after Freddie Gray died in police custody, some worship leaders at my church wrote a song based on Psalm 22. We sang it together the next Sunday, and it was a really powerful experience of communal lament, of crying out in pain together."[11]

Another example of how to express one's lament for injustice is found in this speech attributed to Chief Seattle, a Suquamish and Duwamish chief. Although the origins of the speech are debated, since it was later constructed from notes taken by an observer, it can still be found on the Suquamish tribe's website. It is a bittersweet cry for the respect of Native peoples and the role of the land in carrying on the memory of lament:

Every part of this soil is sacred in the estimation of my people. Every hillside, every valley, every plain and grove, has been hallowed by some sad or happy event in days long vanished. Even the rocks, which seem to be dumb and dead as they swelter in the sun along the silent shore, thrill with memories of stirring events connected with the lives of my people, and the very dust upon which you now stand responds more lovingly to their footsteps than yours, because it is rich with the blood of our ancestors, and our bare feet are conscious of the sympathetic touch. Our departed braves, fond mothers, glad, happy hearted maidens, and even the little children who lived here and rejoiced here for a brief season, will love these somber solitudes and at eventide they greet shadowy returning spirits.[12]

The circumstances of life will cause us to lament if we allow ourselves to really feel their weight. And it is by learning to lament that we will find the urgency to get involved and move toward the activation stage of reconciliation. I am convinced that, using lament, emerging leaders can enter the experience of racial suffering, oppression, and perseverance by people of color in the United States and others around the globe. As reconcilers, we must connect to and identify with the suffering of people around us. When we do this, the work of reconciliation can begin.

Nehemiah seemed to understand the power of lament, and he became the embodiment of what it means to lament. He trusted God to hear his prayer and to intervene. In doing so, he admitted that he was incapable of addressing the pressing issues of Jerusalem by himself. Nehemiah prayed for four months, giving himself to a significant time of mourning and crying out to God. He wept as he laid out his petition, pleading for his people and repenting for the sins of his nation. It was in the presence of the Lord, who made a covenant with the people of Israel, that Nehemiah found hope. He believed that God would fulfill the plans and purposes that were promised, which gave him faith and compelled him to act.

Similarly, this younger generation of Christians, in order to lead with empathy and compassion, must develop the ability to lament. This spiritual resource is action oriented and has the power to galvanize reconciliation leaders to work in solidarity with others. When this occurs, they will be able to leverage their collective power and work together for meaningful change. Their belief in a God who hears will give them the hope and strength to keep working to make the world better.

THREE

Pursue Proximity to the Problem

When I reached Jerusalem and had been there for three days, I set out at night, taking only a few people with me. I didn't tell anyone what my God was prompting me to do for Jerusalem, and the only animal I took was the one I rode. I went out by night through the Valley Gate past the Dragon's Spring to the Dung Gate so that I could inspect the walls of Jerusalem that had been broken down, as well as its gates, which had been destroyed by fire.

Then I went on to the Spring Gate and to the King's Pool. Since there was no room for the animal on which I was riding to pass, I went up by way of the valley by night and inspected the wall. Then I turned back and returned by entering through the Valley Gate.

—Nehemiah 2:11–15

Not long after I moved to Chicago, Ray Bakke, an urban missiologist, took a small group of urban leaders, myself included, on a pilgrimage to learn the stories behind Chicago's development as a major metropolitan city. As he took us around the city, pointing out notable sites and landmarks, we began to realize that things are not always the way they appear. When people move to a new location or experience a new neighborhood, they may assume that what they see is the way things have always been. Each place we encounter has been formed by events and circumstances that preceded the moment of our visitation. There is always a story under the story—a deeper and more complex narrative about how things became the way they are. Uncovering this story is the interrogative work of exegeting our context, something that Nehemiah embarked on when he rode the donkey around the ruins of Jerusalem, described in the passage above, and that Bakke wanted to teach us on that ride around Chicago.

Bakke took our team down the Dan Ryan Expressway, a major freeway that traverses the length of Chicago from the north to the south. As we were driving, Bakke pointed out a curve in the freeway. As we approached that portion of the road, we noticed a large Catholic church that diverted the freeway from its straight route. Bakke asked, "Why is this freeway heading straight toward the church?" It was his way of pushing us to be more observant about what we saw.

Then he told us this story: Richard J. Daley was the mayor of Chicago from 1955 until his death in 1976. Known as "the last of the big city bosses," Daley was a powerful man. Nothing happened without Mayor Daley's knowledge and, in most cases, approval. Chicago, like so many cities during the time of his administration, was undergoing significant development and growth. During his tenure, a great deal of construction took place, including the Dan Ryan Expressway and the intentional placement of housing projects that lined both sides of the highway. To facilitate this development, the city often relied on a process called eminent domain, whereby the city had the power to acquire private property for public use, such as to build a major highway. The compensation did little to stop the devastation in many communities. Neighborhoods were destroyed as houses were leveled, businesses bulldozed, and churches demolished to make way for "progress." However, in this case, the church remained and the highway diverted. Bakke probed us further: "How did it get that way and why?"

It turns out that the Catholic church at the turn on the expressway refused to move—even under pressure from the city of Chicago. That church stood firm that they did not want to destroy their parish or the ability for families to walk to the church safely. This church said no to the freeway, so the freeway had to go around the church.

Bakke continued sharing the story that in response to the affront by the church, in refusing to acquiesce to the city's demands, Mayor Daley authorized the construction of a subsidized housing development immediately behind the church and filled it with poor Black people. Over time, due to multiple factors, including significant disinvestment from the city, the development became notorious for gang violence, crime, and drugs—all of which occurred just beyond the walls of the church. Riding by, under casual observance, we could have made all kinds of observations about the church and its surrounding community, and likely none of them would have included the church's stand against the Dan Ryan Freeway and Mayor Daley.

Bakke taught us how to conduct a cultural exegesis. He wanted us to understand that the story didn't begin with a church in "the hood." As he shared its true history, we began to see how this curved freeway was telling us why this church and the surrounding community was in decline and plagued by crime. Bakke told us a cautionary tale about a powerful mayor who used impoverished, marginalized people to spite a Catholic church that dared to defy him. That housing project was never built to thrive. That church was never meant to survive the construction of the freeway. Things were not the way they were by accident; an untold intentionality contributed to the devastation we witnessed. When we explored beneath the surface, there was more to the story than what initially appeared.

This experience with Bakke made such an impact on my approach to engaging with new communities that I now take my reconciliation students on an annual excursion in Seattle to learn how to perform a cultural exegesis of their context. No matter where they live after graduating, my students will need to have the ability to understand the true story of their communities. The bus we use to ride around town is like a cocoon for the students' transformation. As we travel the city, I ask probing questions and challenge the students to look beneath the surface to explore how places are formed and shaped, not just by the terrain and buildings but also by the people, the culture, and the shared history. This pilgrimage provides the context for listening to the stories that the land tells. The land bears witness to how people, made in the image of God, are being treated. This mobile, sociocultural history lesson helps these students prepare to leave college with an awareness of how to become part of the new places they will inhabit. Proximity is a key component in this type of educational experience.

Getting Close to the Problem

Nehemiah had to get physically proximate to the trouble of his people. He went on a pilgrimage to personally survey the situation in Jerusalem. With the permission of King Artaxerxes, he traveled eight hundred miles from Persia to his home country.

Being in solidarity with others demands getting close to the problem, seeking to really understand the issue, and acting to help address the situation. We must go to where the walls are "broken down" and "the gates have been burned with fire" (Neh. 1:3). Our proximity breeds care while our distance from people breeds fear. Find the people who are hurting and listen to them. You can't tell the story or empathize with people if you don't know the story. You cannot fully know the story until you get close to it.

It is the ministry of presence that is needed now. We must ask ourselves, What does it mean for the church to show up? Perhaps it will entail door-to-door listening to hear people's fears, perspectives, concerns, and hopes for their community. To be well-informed we might need to survey those in the community to learn when something is statistically relevant. And we must be present and build trust to bring as many people's concerns, voices, and perspectives together as possible.

In sociological terms, this is called "ethnography." Ethnography requires proximity to what is happening. This means getting close enough to have your own aha moments. These moments allow you to make sense of the situation and provide a greater understanding of how circumstances got the way they are. Nehemiah was not required to make the sojourn to Jerusalem to assess the condition of his community firsthand. He could have remained in comfort and lamented the plight of his people from afar. Instead, he made the commitment to see the problem for himself. An ethnographic inquiry explores how people live and make sense of their lives with one another in specific places. This research describes people in their context based on experiences, interactions, observations, and sensory information. It allows us to capture the story—to identify the different characters and document the sights and sounds that help us better understand the narrative of a particular context.

The focus of ethnography might be on people and the meaning they produce through everyday interactions, or it could be the organizational logic that guides their activities. Ultimately, the goal of ethnography is learning from a community and allowing solutions to come from within that community, instead of bringing answers from the outside and imposing them on a context or a particular group of people. Sociologists have found that immersion in colonized communities of color is the only method that reshapes people's worldview by seeing the underside of empire and its impact. As Soong-Chan Rah says, "Without rigorous cultural exegesis and social analysis, those who move to the city to be urban missionaries are simply urban colonizers."[1]

To immerse ourselves within a new culture, we will have to prepare ourselves mentally and emotionally, and we must learn to exegete our context, as I learned to do many years ago in Chicago with Bakke.

We must start with an open mind and be willing to look at things with fresh eyes. Practicing objectivity is key. Nehemiah arose in the night and viewed the ruins of the walls to determine the appropriate method of repair. He set out from the west side of the city, then turned toward the south, continuing counterclockwise around the rubble of the city walls before finally returning to his starting point. For the first time, he saw with his own eyes what had been reported to him. Like Nehemiah, we must get close enough to survey the situation and understand the story and the context for ourselves.

To engage another culture, we must eliminate preconceived notions that can keep us from getting to the truth. When Nehemiah arrived, he didn't talk to people, and he didn't take a large group with him, lest he be influenced by their perception of the situation. He needed to see it for himself. Sometimes the smallest observation can be an important part of a culture. When engaged in this process, it is critical to pay attention to all our senses and take notes about what we observe.

Ethnography is not just about the study of other people and places. The observer is also part of the process. It is crucial for the observer to study their own reactions and insights when participating in ethnographic work. If we are in a situation where a notepad or recorder are not practical or may have a negative effect on interacting with people, we will need to capture what we've observed in a journal as soon as possible. Journaling can put us in a reflective mode, which forces us to be more precise about our thoughts rather than simply mulling over ideas in our head.

Journaling provides the atmosphere for the intersection of ministry experience and personal reflection. We can't connect our story with those of others if we don't know our story. Nehemiah embarked upon his pilgrimage knowing his own story and the story of his people. We know from the sadness he expressed to King Artaxerxes that Nehemiah was connected to the plight of his people in Jerusalem.

Nehemiah undertook a precise and calculated information-gathering effort before he started working. While it is vitally important to do our homework first, we cannot rely only on sensory information. Nehemiah did not act immediately after his careful examination of the situation. He suspended his plan for God's plan. While reconciliation may have many strategic components, it is not a project or a strategy with a timeline—it is a spirituality. We must start with vision and discernment, which come from God. We discover what we must do, then discern the timing of when we should do it. When discernment is coupled with vision and proximity, our work will have credibility.

Demonstrating Concern

Proximity is important not just because it allows us to gain greater understanding of the situation; it also demonstrates our concern to those in need. I learned this firsthand when I attended the court proceedings in a case involving students at Seattle Pacific University. My graduate assistant was among a group of students who had sued the board of trustees, challenging how the trustees enforced the university's human sexuality conduct policy, specifically as it relates to the LGBTQ+ community. When I arrived, the courtroom was packed, so I sat in the hallway outside with about twenty-five students and alumni. The students were alleging that board members purposely misled students and professors to believe in a good-faith attempt to collaborate and cocreate a policy that would represent everyone's perspective.

As I sat in the hallway and listened to the proceedings on Zoom, I gained a deeper understanding than if I had heard about the proceedings secondhand. For example, I was struck by the board's selection of a female attorney, which appeared to be an attempt to give credibility to the board's position that they were not discriminating against people based on their gender or sexuality but instead were adhering to their religious beliefs. I was deeply saddened as I listened to her construct the argument that seemed to me to disregard students' humanity. I didn't see concern for the real challenges and complexities these young people face on a daily basis. My heart broke as I imagined the impact of those words on the students who were plaintiffs in the lawsuit but also on those who gathered with me in the courtroom hallway, as well as those students of the university who were not present.

The attorney for the plaintiffs presented the argument from the students' perspective. He explained that this was not a legal dispute about religious beliefs or the university's human sexuality policy. Instead, the students' argument centered on what they perceived to be deceit and misrepresentation by the board. The students' lawyer convincingly argued that the board never intended to operate in good faith with the rest of the campus community. Instead, the students' position was that they were promised a lie from the beginning.

I was glad to be sitting in the hallway watching these court proceedings in proximity to other students instead of watching from my office. I looked at them and I thought to myself, "This is about their lives!" It hurt to watch these young queer people enduring adults' arguments about their lives as if they did not exist as human beings. As I took it all in, I realized how being at the courthouse helped me understand the problem better than I ever could if I had been listening from another, more comfortable location.

After hearing both sides, the judge decided that the matter was too important to rule from the bench. As everyone flooded out of the courtroom and into the hallway, I understood the importance for students, especially my graduate assistant, to see me there. When she saw me, we immediately embraced each other tightly. It spoke volumes to her that I was willing to make the effort to physically show up beyond offering words of support. My presence gave credibility to my words; I showed her that I cared about her and by extension the LGBTQ+ community. The fact that I made this a priority and took time out of my week to go downtown to the courthouse meant that I was willing to get close enough to the problem to feel the weight of its implications. My presence bore witness that I really loved these students enough to bring my full self and demonstrate my solidarity with their struggle.

Looking Back to Move Forward

Proximity can be achieved by being physically present in the now, but it can also come from a different kind of journey: visiting a past location to better understand present conditions. The African word *Sankofa* from the Akan tribe in Ghana captures this idea perfectly. It means "looking back to move forward." Sankofa symbolizes the Akan people's quest for knowledge, with the implication that the quest is based on critical examination and an intelligent and patient investigation. The symbol reflecting this concept is a mythical bird with its feet firmly planted forward but its head facing backward. This figure portrays the Akan community's belief that the past serves as a guide for planning the future. The wisdom that we glean from the past enables and empowers us to build a strong future. For the Akan people, there must be movement and new learning as time passes. As this forward march proceeds, the knowledge of the past must never be forgotten.

Sankofa can provide an important methodology for ethnography. I experienced this when I embarked on a Sankofa excursion with a diverse group of women and visited the house of Harriet Tubman in Auburn, New York. As we stood on the ground where she lived after making her way to freedom, her story became much more real to us. It helped us humanize her, and we became part of her story. We had walked on the land and touched her DNA in the world. In doing so, the embodiment gap was closed between the story we'd heard and the truth of what really happened.

For example, I'd never known that Harriet Tubman owned a house. This knowledge gives me hope and courage to believe that if Harriet made it, we would also make it. The power of pilgrimage is that two stories now intersect. She becomes part of my story and transforms it. The end of Harriet's story and her faith shows me that we get to have stability and exercise agency over our own lives. Her extraordinary leadership reminds us that if Harriet struggled mightily to achieve freedom and flourishing, with all the obstacles stacked against her, we can do the same in our own time. If Harriet made it to freedom and lived in her own house, then we, too, can lead our communities to freedom and collective thriving, where homes, lives, and futures can be rebuilt.

As we took time to remember our past, telling the truth of our history and the story of the land, we poured out libations in honor of Tubman's legacy. In that sacred ceremony we looked back and asked questions, such as, Who do we see as fully human? We discussed the confinement and control of Black and Brown bodies on the land. We stood on the ground and acknowledged white men's distorted justification for the genocide of Native peoples ("We want your land to prop up our economy"); for the enslavement of Black people ("We want your body to prop up our economy"); for the internment of Asian people ("You are almost human and present a constant threat, and we must fight against you").

We agreed that race, citizenship, and gender are intricately connected. In addition, we noted that race and gender are always used by white supremacist patriarchy to create divisions and pit people against each other. All this is done to maintain their power. As women in solidarity with each other, we pledged to resist and heal this divide moving forward. A woman from West Papua summarized her newfound understanding of the impact of colonization on her knowledge of God when she said, "I realize that I've been reading the gospel using someone else's glasses." Cultural exegesis allows us to remove the glasses of those in power and equips us with the ability to view reality through the lens of truth. And we already know what happens with the truth . . . it sets you free.

Organize a Diverse Coalition

The officials didn't know where I had gone or what I was doing. I hadn't yet told the Jews, the priests, the officials, the officers, or the rest who were to do the work. So I said to them, "You see the trouble that we're in: Jerusalem is in ruins, and its gates are destroyed by fire! Come, let's rebuild the wall of Jerusalem so that we won't continue to be in disgrace."

—Nehemiah 2:16–17

Organizing is a form of leadership that calls people to work together because they have a desperate need for each other. Disparate groups align as they realize that their survival is connected to each other. They come together across racial, cultural, socioeconomic, and global differences because it is in the best interest of every person involved. Reconciliation cannot be done in isolation; it must be done in community. It is in community where we find mutuality. The fire for change is reignited as we work together. We need solidarity for communal healing to occur. We are stronger together. To be successful in reaching our goals, we must establish trusting relationships that enable us to work well together.

Over the years, I have sought to learn the principles and strategies of organizing people so I could help Christian leaders mobilize their churches and organizations to actively work for reconciliation in their local contexts. In order to deepen my understanding about community organizing, I took a class with Marshall Ganz, the Rita T. Hauser Senior Lecturer in Leadership, Organizing, and Civil Society at the Kennedy School of Government at Harvard University. Ganz was introduced to community organizing during the civil rights movement. He was an undergraduate student at Harvard and dropped out to participate in the Montgomery bus boycott. After the assassination of Martin Luther King Jr., he worked on the staff of the United Farm Workers movement under the leadership of Cesar Chavez for sixteen years. For over three decades Chavez led the first successful farm workers union in American history, achieving dignity, respect, fair wages, medical coverage, pension benefits, and humane living conditions for hundreds of thousands of farm workers. Afterward, Ganz became a trainer and organizer for political campaigns, unions, and nonprofit groups before returning to Harvard, where he earned his PhD in sociology. Ganz is also credited with orchestrating the successful grassroots organizing model for Barack Obama's presidential campaign in 2008.

In our first session, Ganz explained the purpose of the class: to create social change through collective action. He asked, "How did you learn to ride a bike?" Several people responded and said that they got on the bike and their dad, family member, or some other adult held on to the seat to help steady them; then they began to pedal and got their balance, and eventually the grown-up let go. Initially, they felt euphoric because they were so proud that they were doing it. But then they would get wobbly and fall off the bike. After making sure they were okay, the mentor would tell them to get back up, brush themselves off, and try again. Over time, they would become more confident and steadier until one day they were finally and joyfully riding the bike!

When everyone finished sharing, Ganz said, "Did you notice that nobody said they read a book or took a class to learn how to ride a bike?" For everyone in the class, it was a trial-and-error process until at some point they learned how to ride the bike . . . by actually riding it. He went on to explain that this course would be the same. We were to become what we want to be by doing it. You become an organizer by organizing. This would be a class in practice, and it would require that we try new things, risk failure, and be willing to step outside our comfort zone. He told us that we were all going to get on the bike, knowing we might fall. He encouraged us to get back up and try it again.

In our next class session, we slowly and courageously got on the bike and learned that to organize people, there are three stories that we must be able to tell. The first is the "story of self." This is our personal narrative about why this social, racial, cultural, political, or environmental issue is important. We must ask ourselves, Why do I feel called to get actively involved?

After we clearly understand why we are personally invested, we want to tell people about the "story of us." We talk about why we believe other people should also get involved in addressing the problem that we are concerned about. Telling this story requires being able to share what the problem has to do with other people and why they should

73

also be concerned. The question we should ask is, Why do I want to call people to work together on this issue and why is it in their collective best self-interest to do so?

Finally, we must be able to tell the "story of now." We strongly tell our listeners that there is a sense of urgency that demands coming together at this moment to do something about the problem.

These three compelling stories come together to inform and clarify the methodology to organize people to work together toward the common good. It is imperative to know our own story of self to understand and explain why we personally care and feel passionate about this issue. People with a strong commitment to their community, organization, or values will have the most success in establishing themselves as trustworthy leaders, calling people to join this important effort. We share why we believe other people should be concerned about the problem. Our final appeal is to ask people to use their resources, energy, gifts, skills, and time to do something about this issue because this is a story of now.

A Community Effort

Nehemiah knew that repairing the wall was a community effort. He started developing his story of self when he heard the news about his people while he was in the king's palace. Once he arrived at Jerusalem, he continued the development by enlisting a few key advisers in the initial inspection. He then surveyed the ruined walls for himself. He needed to know the condition of the walls, where he could rebuild the walls on the existing foundation, where he had to start from scratch and construct something new, and the accuracy of the intelligence he had received.

Only when he had the information he needed, when he developed his own story, did he call the people together to share the story of us. He was honest about how bad things were. He told them it would be a demanding job: the circuit of the walls was more than a mile long and the new wall needed to be three or four feet thick and fifteen to twenty feet high. Nehemiah told them they would have to give it their best effort, and he impressed upon them the necessity to rebuild. Finally, he shared the story of now by declaring that rebuilding the wall was God's mission and, therefore, God would give them the victory.

Nehemiah was an effective organizer. He knew that the task was too large for any single individual, that he would need everyone's support and participation. Nehemiah needed all hands on deck: men and women, young and old, skilled and unskilled, experienced and inexperienced, working class and rulers. Nehemiah shared his vision with the entire community—it was a diverse coalition of people. There are thirty-eight distinct people listed and over forty work teams who are recorded as laboring together to repair the wall. People with differing gifts and trades were involved, including priests, Levites, civil leaders, perfumers, goldsmiths, merchants, and temple assistants.

Nehemiah was also strategic in his work assignments. He assigned many workers their tasks near to their homes. This was a wise decision because they each had a personal interest in their section. Priests rebuilt the sheep gate since they had a particular interest in that location because of the temple sacrifices. All the people were invested in rebuilding the wall because of their personal interest, but they were also keenly aware of their story of us: everyone was vulnerable without it. In places where people would generally be divided, they collectively worked together because they needed each other.

Heather McGhee, an expert in economic and social policy, emphatically makes this point in her book *The Sum of Us*:

> The old zero-sum paradigm is not just counterproductive; it's a lie. . . . To this day, the wealthy and the powerful are still selling the zero-sum story for their own profit, hoping to keep people with much in common from making common cause with one another. But not everyone is buying it. Everywhere I went, I found that the people who had replaced the zero sum with a new formula of cross-racial solidarity had found the key to unlocking what I began to call a "Solidarity Dividend," from higher wages to cleaner air, made possible through collective action.[1]

If today's emerging leaders are going to bring people together, everyone involved must see how the work brings good for everyone. When racially, culturally, ethnically, socially, and economically diverse people come together to work on a common issue, they must understand that it is for our collective well-being. Audre Lorde said, "Without community there is no liberation."[2]

The notion of collective well-being runs contrary to the competitive zero-sum belief that dominates our culture. This belief has led to a pervasive "us versus them" mentality in our society, which divides people based on race. McGhee continues,

> The logical extension of the zero-sum story is that a future without racism is something white people should fear, because there will be nothing good for them in it. They should be arming themselves (as they have been in record numbers, "for protection," since the Obama presidency) because demographic change will end in a dog-eat-dog race war. Obviously, this is not the story we want to tell. It's not even what we

believe. The same research I found showing that white people increasingly see the world through a zero-sum prism showed that Black people do not. African Americans just don't buy that our gain has come at the expense of white people. And time and time and time again, history has shown that we're right. The civil rights victories that were so bitterly opposed in the South ended up being a boon for the region, resulting in stronger local economies and more investments in infrastructure and education.[3]

Educational parity, environmental justice, access to quality health care, and economic equity are things that all people should care about, but to achieve them requires work and collective effort. Like Nehemiah, after we decide what structures need to be repaired, we must determine who is going to fix them. We must determine to whom we are going to tell our story. We begin to grapple with logistical questions, such as, Who are we looking for? Who are the people invested in this work? Who are the people who want to see this place thrive because they've got a stake in the game? Who do we notice always being invited and who's not been invited before?

Sadly, Christians are often not invited because they're not perceived as trustworthy partners in the work of repairing broken structures. Our reputation has been ruined. Many people are convinced that there is no way that the call to justice and being a Christian go together. One of my students experiences this type of judgment on a regular basis. She explained that every time somebody asks her whether her faith acts as a hurdle that she must get past in order to advocate for justice, she determinedly responds, "I'm not getting past it. I'm still deeply Christian. In fact, it's my faith that motivates me to do this work." She further explained that she "wants more people to ask those questions. At the very least, if they are asking questions, it opens up an opportunity to explain how Christianity can lead people to justice, not away from it."

This example demonstrates that Christianity is often conflated with right-wing, ultra-conservative American politics and is considered the source of, instead of the solution to, many of society's biggest problems. When evangelical Christians align themselves with white supremacy, capitalism, patriarchy, and other harmful American ideologies, it demonstrates the degree to which the church has been corrupted like so many other institutions.

This disconnect is why community organizing is necessary to reclaim our Christian credibility and the reputation of people of faith in social activism. There are many people who organize communities around various justice issues who are incredible Christians. I believe rebuilding Christianity's reputation requires going back to the biblical foundations of community. Martin Luther King Jr. was right when he said, "If the church does not recapture its prophetic zeal, it will become an irrelevant social club without moral or spiritual authority."[4]

The church can recapture its prophetic zeal to rebuild broken systems and structures that nurture diverse coalitions. Our response must be to organize a multiracial, multiethnic coalition that will use its collective voice and vote so that all people are free to reach their full, God-given potential. David Leong argues in his book *Race and Place: How Urban Geography Shapes the Journey to Reconciliation* that "to reshape our cities and neighborhoods into places of 'divine belonging,' we must be Christian in the ways we locate our lives together with other people."[5] He warns us that "when we only or even primarily experience belonging in homogeneity—racial, cultural, religious, or otherwise—then we are tragically missing out and falling short of the deeply transformative divine community that must accompany authentic Christian discipleship."[6] By building diverse coalitions, we are also rebuilding what it truly means to be Christian.

Organization is required to build a diverse coalition. In order to be effective, there must be a critical mass of people who are concerned and committed to doing something about the identified problem. This requires strategic leadership. Sometimes leaders with vision lack the ability to implement that vision. In that context, people will become frustrated with repeated pleas to embrace a vision that they view as unrealistic. At other times there are hard-working leaders who immerse themselves in all sorts of activity but have no clear vision of where they're going. We need both vision and action. A Japanese proverb says, "Vision without action is a daydream. Action without vision is a nightmare."

I have found that most people are stronger in one than the other, which is why it's important to seek plurality. The leader must have the vision, but they can't do all the work; it must be a cooperative effort that has buy-in from the people. Organizers must identify, recruit, and develop others for leadership; build community around that leadership; and build power from the resources of that community. Their goal is to organize a community to become a constituency—people able to stand together on behalf of common concerns. Organizers must ask these three questions: Who are my people? What is their urgent problem? How can they turn their resources into the power to solve their problem? True leaders answer these questions in dialogue with their constituency by building relationships, telling stories, devising strategy, designing structure, and taking action.

To be a true leader, you must first listen to God and get the vision firmly implanted before you are prepared to face the inevitable opposition that will try to discourage you from the task. Have ready answers to the basic questions to show that you have done your homework. Know what resources and materials will be needed for the construction and how you plan to obtain those resources. Create a plan, but also face the reality that there will always be a degree of uncertainty while doing this work.

I learned this when I heard Marshall Ganz say in class, "Leadership is about accepting responsibility for enabling others to achieve a shared purpose in the face of uncertainty." Uncertainty requires adaptive leadership: not so much performing known tasks well but learning which tasks are needed and how to perform them well. In the face of uncertainty, the world needs leaders who sincerely want to make a change, though they may lack experience. Good leadership has the perspective of a learner—one who has learned to ask the right questions—rather than that of a knower—one who thinks they know all the answers. This kind of leadership is a form of practice, not a position or a person, and it can be exercised from any location within or without a structure of authority.

As I neared the end of my community organizing class, I realized that the process was transforming me. Organizing is not just about what we can teach people. It is as much about the change that occurs in the leader doing the organizing. Reconciliation entails learning how stories are made possible by letting our story change the retelling of other people's stories, which creates the possibility for a new outcome. As disparate coalitions are brought together, the structures are repaired and the individuals involved are restored. The work of God includes not just rebuilding the wall but also rebuilding the people. In the rubble of stones and souls, we must leave room for God to work.

FIVE

Repair the Breach Together

So I said to them, "You see the trouble that we're in: Jerusalem is in ruins, and its gates are destroyed by fire! Come, let's rebuild the wall of Jerusalem so that we won't continue to be in disgrace." I told them that my God had taken care of me, and also told them what the king had said to me. "Let's start rebuilding!" they said, and they eagerly began the work.

—Nehemiah 2:17–18

I still remember the first time I met a young man I have fondly nicknamed "Brother Reparations." I was conducting a reconciliation seminar at a church in Seattle, and during the training, this young Black man raised his hand and asked why I didn't speak more about reparations. We began to discuss our viewpoints as the audience listened attentively. After a while, I gave him the microphone so everyone could hear what he had to say. This both surprised and impressed him. We became friendly and started meeting occasionally at various coffee shops to get to know one another better. Every time we met, no matter the topic, the issue of reparations came up. That's why I began calling him Brother Reparations.

Later that year, Bryan Stevenson, founder of the Equal Justice Initiative and author of *Just Mercy: A Story of Justice and Redemption*, came to speak at a church in Seattle. The event was sold out, but Brother Reparations was part of the sponsoring organization and got me a ticket. At the end of the presentation, when the time came for questions from the audience, the very first person to raise his hand was Brother Reparations. I nudged a person I knew sitting next to me and said, "I don't know what he's going to ask, but whatever it is, it's got something to do with reparations!" Sure enough, when Stevenson called on him, he stood to his feet and loudly asked, "Mr. Stevenson, do you believe in reparations?"

I will never forget Stevenson's answer. He said something to this effect: Of course I do! But anybody can write a check. Real reparations would be to fix what was actually broken. For example, Black people in this country were denied the right to vote. White people brutalized, terrorized, and killed Black people for trying to vote for over a century. So, to repair that, white Americans would automatically give all African Americans the right to vote on their eighteenth birthday. In fact, if you are an elderly African American, they would pick you up and drive you to the polls to vote. Now that would repair what was really broken![1]

My mind was reeling as I left that presentation. While driving home, a Scripture verse suddenly came to mind that I hadn't thought about in years: "Your ancient ruins shall be rebuilt; you shall raise up the foundations of many generations; you shall be called the repairer of the breach, the restorer of streets to live in" (Isa. 58:12 NRSV). That night, I became aware that reparations must be part of reconciliation. As Christ followers, we are supposed to restore safety on our streets so people can travel, build houses, and make their home there. That's what we're called to be and do as God's people! We are called to be the repairers of the breach.

I am convinced that reconciliation and reparations are two sides of the same coin—they are inseparable. It was never supposed to be a choice between one or the other. Reconciliation is both relational and systemic; it involves forgiveness, repentance, and justice that transforms broken systems. Reconciliation embraces other people and values their humanity, and if we value someone's humanity, it requires that we care about the systems and structures that impact their lives and seek to repair those that harm them. Disappointingly, reconciliation has been reduced to multiculturalism and racial unity that ignores these historical realities and social differences that require people of color to assimilate to dominant cultural norms. The restorative power of reparations, which requires that we go beyond just relationships and repair broken systems, has been completely omitted from most Christian reconciliation work. Those systemic problems remain broken as the horrific truth about the enslavement, economic exploitation, rape, and trauma committed against Indigenous people and African Americans continues to be buried, ignored, diminished, and rejected by politicians, academic institutions, civic leaders, and religious organizations. There is power in controlling the narrative—it is the ability to control reality.

Dominique Gilliard, author of *Subversive Witness: Scripture's Call to Leverage Privilege*, makes this point: "Unbridled privilege emboldens immaturity, trivializes oppression, and derails our pursuit of shalom. When we are not honest about what divides us, reconciliation becomes a façade for sustaining the status quo, and the body of Christ becomes a place where 'Peace, peace,' is proclaimed when there is no peace."[2] This privileged audacity has caused a disconnect between reconciliation and the way it is enacted by many white evangelicals, who seem to have co-opted the term to mean a color-blind unity that avoids active accountability to make amends for the racial injustices of the past and the ways they have benefited from those inequities today.

Christians must tell the truth about our racial history and what is broken in our society. Those who have been harmed have become increasingly insistent that apologies without honesty and meaningful recompense are insufficient. Reparations supporters are ready to move past debate: it is time to make amends and tell the truth. Not only for the sake of those who have been disenfranchised by these great injustices but also for the sake of those who have benefited from these wrongs. White Americans must commit to reparations because the truth will also make *them* free. Making reparations allows white Americans to reclaim their humanity by releasing the guilt and shame they carry, consciously or unconsciously. The past is present almost everywhere, whether or not we acknowledge it, and it will continue to inform the future. We are currently facing the reality that an entire generation may be misinformed about the true devastation of racism and slavery. Without those stories, we will never understand the depth of the harm done to everyone. Reconciliation, for past, present, and future generations, is impossible without the recognition that slavery was abhorrent and that substantive apologies that lead to repair are necessary.

Without that, we are facing the prospect of a generation being misled about the true history of slavery and discrimination, and therefore they may be doomed to repeat it.

It is disturbing that we are living in a time when book bans are at an all-time high in the United States.[3] Florida and Texas remain at the top of the list of states banning the most books, followed closely by South Carolina, Missouri, and Utah.[4] Although individuals and coordinated group efforts on the ground have led to book bans, state-level legislation has amplified and encouraged greater overreach of the government into school libraries. The books being banned across the US remain primarily those by and about people of color and queer people. I was shocked to learn that a book by civil rights activist Ruby Bridges, who at six years old became the first Black child to desegregate an all-white Louisiana school, was banned from schools. In response, Bridges said that a conversation about banning books is long overdue: "Let's have it, but it must include all books. If we are to ban books from being too truthful, then surely we must ban books that distort or omit the truth."[5]

The unwillingness to educate children about the truth of history has dire consequences for them, especially when they go to college. As a professor of reconciliation studies, I have heard countless white students in my introductory class tearfully ask, "How did I not know this? How did I graduate from high school at the top of my class and never learn anything about how racial injustices have shaped the very structures of our society that still exist today?" They are often angry and confused, doubting themselves, their parents, and the value of their education. That's why parents who refuse to allow their children to learn about and grapple with the reality of our nation's history are doing their children a great disservice. Parents are not educating children to know the truth about the complex issues they will face in the world around them.

I witnessed the powerful outcome of truth-telling at a conference for Christian college administrators where John DeGioia, former president of Georgetown University, was the opening speaker. In his message, he humbly and honestly shared how his academic institution had intentionally dealt with its racist history. He told the audience how a collection of Georgetown professors, students, alumni, and genealogists uncovered the dark history of how the nation's most prominent Jesuit priests, who ran the school in the early nineteenth century, owned 272 enslaved African men, women, and children. To secure their future as an academic institution, Jesuit leaders sold these enslaved human beings in 1838 to raise money for Georgetown University. In response to learning this history, students at Georgetown voted to increase their tuition to benefit the descendants of the 272 enslaved Africans whom the Jesuit priests sold. Together with the board of directors, administrators, staff, faculty, and students, the Georgetown community courageously confronted the moral question, What is owed to the descendants of slaves who were sold to help ensure the college's survival? Their answer was decided in a groundbreaking vote to create a fund. In 2016, President DeGioia announced that descendants of the enslaved people owned by the Maryland Province of Jesuits would receive preferential admission consideration at Georgetown as a means of repair and reconciliation. In 2020, the student body created a reparations fund for the descendants of the enslaved people to attend Georgetown. In addition, the university renamed two buildings on campus that had been named for the school presidents who organized the sale of the 272 enslaved Black people. This example of reparations for slavery by a prominent Catholic university could be a model for other academic institutions to follow.

Christians must define reparations to set up the broader policy work and the localized healing and repair that must be done. The following definition by Mark Labberton provides a holistic understanding of what this work entails: "Reparations . . . refers to a range of personal, institutional, or governmental acts that seek to redress, repair, and compensate victims and heirs for the unjust taking of life, family, dignity, time, labor, property, and hope—primarily in relation to the colonizing degradation and abuse of Indigenous people and of enslaved Africans in the United States."[6] I appreciate this definition because it clarifies that reparations is not strictly about money or financial restitution. Holistic repair must also include addressing the legacy of enslavement and all the harm that has impacted the lives of Black people to this day. Repair can only result from honestly facing the truth of what happened in the past and seeking to make it right in the present.

We won't be able to heal as a nation until we truthfully deal with the reality of our collective history. Bryan Stevenson says, "We have committed ourselves in this country to silence about our history, to ignorance about our history, to denying our history. And that's the first part of this relationship that has to be repaired. We've got to be willing now to talk honestly about who we are and how we got here."[7] Where we begin the story matters.

Reparations Requires More

Enslavement and related profit-making activities persisted for centuries and continue today, and so we need institutional and governmental acts to address the harm that has been done. Apologies with meaningful recompense are overdue. Unfortunately, in the US, two federal reparations bills have stalled. New Jersey and New York launched studies on the impacts of slavery, but calls for reparations have generated significant misinformation and complaints of racial bias and discrimination against non-Black residents. This seems to be rooted in a historical discrepancy about who is deserving of human rights. For example, public acts of violence that were obvious and undeniable in well-established communities are impossible to erase. These racial hate crimes perpetrated against people who lost their lives, homes, and livelihood demanded the need to be acknowledged and compensated for. Two examples of this type of reparations were made to Japanese Americans who suffered imprisonment in intern-ment camps and the descendants of the Black community of Rosewood, Florida.

In 1988, President Ronald Reagan signed the Civil Liber-ties Act, providing $1.2 billion ($20,000 per person) and an apology to each of the approximately 60,000 living Japanese Americans who suffered the racial trauma and dehumaniza-tion of being interned during World War II. There was also the need to make amends for an atrocity that occurred in January 1923 in the central Florida town of Rosewood. Over the course of a week, Black people were murdered and their thriving community was destroyed by a white mob driven by racial hatred. Over seventy years later, attempting to make restitution, the state of Florida acknowledged the devastat-ing crime in 1994 and approved $2.1 million for the living survivors.

In these cases, the people and communities harmed were identified and the financial recompense necessary to address the horrible injustice they suffered was quantified. However, the sweeping centuries of enslavement for Black people are so vast that it is almost impossible to reckon with the devastation wreaked on countless human lives and families. Labberton rightly states, "The horrific injustices perpetrated against Indigenous people and enslaved Africans are so extreme, so public, and so multigenerational in their devastation, that reparations seem to be closer to a minimum, not a maximum, response within God's redemptive justice and healing."[8]

Reparations will require more active involvement from us as Christians. God's character and actions call God's people to act justly toward others. The theological argument for reparations must be firmly rooted in who we understand God to be. Through the pursuit of reparations people can heal their inner wounds and reclaim their deadened humanity. In making amends, one can live more fully into their humanity—in other words, become more alive. It gives all people an opportunity to experience healing and become who God created them to be.

We must participate with God in this reparational process, although many people seem to have given up hope that reparations are possible. I understand their pessimism, which likely stems from the lack of truth-telling they've experienced from those in power as well as the arbitrary and discretionary application of justice in this country, especially in Black and Brown communities. Former US president Barack Obama identifies with people's distrust of empty political rhetoric about America's commitment to invest in racial equity. He says:

I'm not so optimistic as to think that you would ever be able to garner a majority of an American Congress that would make those kinds of investments above and beyond the kinds of investments that could be made in a progressive program for lifting up all people. So, to restate it: I have much more confidence in my ability, or any president or any leader's ability, to mobilize the American people around a multiyear, multibillion-dollar investment to help every child in poverty in this country than I am in being able to mobilize the country around providing a benefit specific to African Americans as a consequence of slavery and Jim Crow. Now, we can debate the justness of that. But I feel pretty confident in that assessment politically.[9]

It seems that former president Obama is saying that he had to navigate many obstacles impeding progress toward achieving reparations. Instead of getting stuck in resistance from those who opposed his efforts, he maneuvered legislation for children in poverty to achieve economic equity. Similarly, we might be called to work for leveling the playing field while we continue to fight for reparations. When unjust institutions and systems attempt to impede our progress, we can go directly to the people. Like Nehemiah, we can help people understand the urgent needs in their local communities and mobilize them to be part of repairing what is broken. We can focus on the results and impact versus how we name the impact. Mobilizing those in a local context can be an extremely effective way to advance the work of social and racial equity in communities, cities, and states around the country.

With this long-term and short-term perspective, committed to the justice we so urgently need and the restorative justice embodied in reparations, we can get to the work of rebuilding. In her book *Dear White Christians*, author Jennifer Harvey says, "An approach to race and racial justice that centers on repair (rather than tolerance, inclusion, appreciation, etc.) is the critical dimension of a reparations paradigm." Reparations supporters have pushed past mere debate and are demanding action. Harvey continues: "Attending to structures for repair and redress—the same structures through which race is constructed, the same structures to which we have different relationships—is the path we need to pursue to live into the reconstructed interracial relationships for which we long."[10]

To accomplish this repair, it is vitally important to identify what needs to be repaired in specific places, because the needs differ. Note, for instance, that the workers in Nehemiah's story were not all doing the same thing at the same time. The people were engaged in different types of work along the wall. Those working for repair are not called to do identical work, nor in identical ways. Instead, each person must participate in this effort based on their unique skills and abilities, and they must leverage their individual platforms and spheres of influence to be successful.

Even now there are many different approaches to repair being led by people in the United States and abroad. For instance, the racial wealth gap is evidence of a broken economic and banking system. Eddie Yoon, founder of Eddie Would Grow, an advisory firm on growth strategy, and Dave Ferguson, the lead pastor of Community Christian Church, a large multisite church outside of Chicago, created a group that seeks to address this problem. The idea came from a report in June 2020, when Netflix announced it was moving 2 percent of its cash, or $100 million, to bolster Black-owned or Black-run banks, allowing those banks to lend more. Together Eddie and Dave started #JusticeDeposits to recapitalize Black and minority-owned banks across the country. They are challenging churches, businesses, and individuals to simply open checking or savings accounts to help Black-owned banks, making funds more accessible to Black and minority families and businesses. Community Christian Church has moved 5 to 10 percent of its cash holdings to Broadway Federal Bank, the largest Black-owned bank in the US after its merger with City First Bank. More faith institutions of all denominations across the nation are starting to follow suit.[11]

Sometimes the system that needs repair is within our own family. I learned about a group called Heirs of Slavery, which encourages wealthy British families who profited from past enslavement to make formal apologies and to seek reparative justice in the former Caribbean colonies.[12] Its cofounders are Laura Trevelyan, a longtime anchor and correspondent with the BBC, and David Lascelles, who is a second cousin of King Charles III and heir to an estate built on earnings from the slave and sugar trades on the island of Barbados. As they both began reckoning with their own family histories, they were shocked and ashamed that their ancestors enslaved Africans across many plantations in the Caribbean. Trevelyan and Lascelles learned that their ancestors earned the equivalent of millions of dollars in compensation when slavery was abolished. Trevelyan donated a portion of her BBC pension to reparations, and she and her family members traveled to Grenada to make a formal apology.[13]

These are only two practical examples of repair in action that represent ways to heal broken structures that impede progress, inclusion, and change. Hopefully, they will help us see that the framework for repair requires those who have benefited from the harm to actively work to fix it. People who are descendants of those who obliterated communities, stole land, and commoditized human life must acknowledge the gravity of those actions in ways that are sufficient to inspire them to make restitution. This must be done under the leadership of and in collaboration with those whose lives have been affected. To actively work to bridge the gap between reconciliation and reparations people must ask:

- What is broken in my city, state, and local community?
- What is at the root of this brokenness?
- What do I and those around me have the capacity to change or address?

We need to seriously and prayerfully consider these questions, because no one can fix everything, but each one of us possesses a unique gift, a sphere of influence, or certain talents that can aid in the work of reparations. You have something that will help repair broken structures that are damaging people's lives. This optimism is balanced by the sobering reality that our acts of repair will never be complete in this broken world. Harvey reminds us, "Work to repair will always be partial." She further explains,

> No act of repair is going to heal the entirety of our racial division and wounds. It certainly won't heal all the harm experienced by and among Black, Latino/a, Native, and Asian American communities. These legacies are long, thick, and wide. At the same time, in any place where racial harm is a reality—which is to say, everywhere—the act of repair is as within reach as simply determining to redistribute resources in response to it; to do so in a manner that seeks, at the same time, to disrupt the systems and policies that keep reproducing such harm and make it lasting and multigenerational; and to do so while clearly naming such work as

a reparations-based response to racial injustice, not a form of charity or social work—and, when pursued by white and colonial-settler people, from a posture of repentance.[14]

Although we may never be able to truly undo the material implications of historical racial injustice, we can show the world what equity and reparations can look like. We must start where we are, at our own location along the "wall" of broken systems. We must be the Nehemiahs declaring the presence of God in this justice work. Then the people can collectively respond, "Let's start rebuilding!"

SIX

Expect External and Internal Opposition

We continued to build the wall. All of it was joined together, and it reached half of its intended height because the people were eager to work. But when Sanballat, Tobiah, the Arabs, the Ammonites, and the people of Ashdod heard that the work on the walls was progressing and the gaps were being closed, they were very angry. They plotted together to come and fight against Jerusalem and to create a disturbance in it.

—Nehemiah 4:6–8

At this point in Nehemiah's rebuilding project, progress on the wall brought out the enemy. Sanballat and Tobiah were rulers in two of the Persian provinces surrounding Judah and were very angry that someone had come to help the Jews. They appeared to be threatened by Nehemiah's success in rebuilding the wall because they did not want Jerusalem to become a strong and well-defended city. When the work began, Sanballat and others taunted and planned an attack on the builders. Unable to dispute Nehemiah's authority, Sanballat became angry, scoffed at the efforts of those "feeble Jews" (4:2), and heckled them while they were working. Sanballat was clearly skeptical that the people could complete the job without help. He and Tobiah considered themselves Israelites, but they did not identify as Jews or Judahites. Sanballat used the term "Jews" as a derogatory label for Nehemiah's group.

Although Sanballat and Tobiah were Yahwists, and Sanballat's daughter even married into a family of the high priest, they also mixed several originally distinct belief systems and traditions to include the worship of other gods. Nehemiah adamantly opposed this type of syncretism. He knew that it constituted the type of spiritual compromise that landed Israel in exile in the first place, and so he resisted all attempts to infiltrate the community. He did not want to repeat the mistakes of the past. Nehemiah took a firm stance against these officials.

The Jewish people were "eager to work" (4:6), but they were exhausted, and Nehemiah understood the vulnerability and exposure that happens in the middle of rebuilding. In an article titled "Lessons from Nehemiah," speaker and writer Carla Gasser rightly observes:

> Halfway points are always critical. On the one hand, we can feel very encouraged when a project is almost completed. Our accomplishments can invigorate and encourage us to keep moving ahead. On the other hand, the middle can also become a place of discouragement and hopelessness as we

realize there is so much further to go. Now throw in a personal attack, and we are vulnerable to burning out, walking away for a while, or leaving the job altogether.[1]

Nehemiah's story exemplifies the inevitable challenges that will come from both external and internal forces, even when working toward a common goal. There will always be setbacks and opposition. Fatigue will come and we will feel discouraged. That's when we must decide not to lose heart or the idealism to keep pushing. Many people will start the work enthusiastically but then burn out. Actively engaging in the work of reconciliation and reparations is often overwhelming. A sincere fire to see change cannot be trusted until it has been challenged—repeatedly. There is no *if* it gets hard—it's *when* it gets hard. There must be a shared community response to meet and overcome this inevitable discouragement.

When Nehemiah saw discouragement, doubt, and fear taking hold of his workers, he acted. Jews from the surrounding area came to Nehemiah and told him about plots against the community, so he created a plan to respond to the rumored threats. He countered the people's distress with action. He spread the people out along the wall and gave them a horn to sound the alarm and call for help in case the enemies attacked. The burden bearers held a weapon in one hand while carrying their load in the other. The builders, needing both hands free, girded a sword on their side. Nehemiah not only organized those working on the wall; he also committed his own resources to guard the community against danger. He provided his own personal retainers, who were constantly armed to guard the community. The horn blower stayed next to Nehemiah, ready to sound a call to gather and fight. The text reports that Nehemiah and others set guards over the building project. Some would work and others would guard. Unfortunately, in any endeavor, there will be opposition, and to be successful, people must work together and protect each other.

Facing Intimidation

When people start making real progress toward repairing broken systems, those in opposition often use intimidation to try and stop the work. This common tactic is used to oppose those working for progress. Even though his enemies cannot stop Nehemiah, they possess power to terrorize him with threats and harassment.

A recent example of intimidation was experienced by Congresswoman Alexandria Ocasio-Cortez. On July 24, 2020, while on the steps of the Capitol Building, she found herself in a heated conversation with Representative Ted Yoho, a Republican from Florida, who reportedly called her "disgusting." He went on to say that she was "out of her freaking mind." When the discussion ended, Yoho allegedly hurled a pair of expletives her way. Yoho later brought up the matter in a speech in the House. In Ocasio-Cortez's response, she said she had planned to ignore the insult—that being a woman had required a lifetime of ignoring such insults—but changed her mind after Yoho brought up the matter himself. "Having been married for 45 years with two daughters, I'm very cognizant of language," Yoho had said, insisting that he'd been misheard and hadn't used the pejorative phrase that a reporter heard him say. While Yoho apologized for the "misunderstanding," he said, "I cannot apologize for my passion or for loving my God, my family, and my country."[2] In a moving speech from the House floor, Congresswoman Ocasio-Cortez responded:

> I do not need Rep. Yoho to apologize to me; clearly, he does not want to. . . . This harm that Mr. Yoho tried to levy at me was not just an incident directed at me. When you do that to anyone, what Mr. Yoho did was give permission to other men to do that to his daughters. . . . I am here to stand up to say that is not acceptable. . . . Having a daughter does not make a man decent. . . . Treating people with dignity and respect makes a decent man. And when a decent man messes up, as we all are bound to do, he . . . does apologize. Not to save face. Not to win a vote. He apologizes genuinely to repair and acknowledge the harm done so that we can all move on.[3]

Like the stance taken by Congresswoman Ocasio-Cortez, Nehemiah countered attempts to intimidate him with courage. The initial opposition came from Sanballat and his associates, and it is easy for a community to believe that all its enemies are coming from the outside. However, enemies can also come from within. Evidently, there was infighting in this postexilic community between those who had remained in the land and the new immigrants who recently returned from exile.

An economic and social crisis had resulted among the builders for several reasons. The first problem was a lack of food supply. The harvest should have yielded an abundance of figs, grapes, and olives, but instead the land experienced a famine. In addition, farmers who were usually tending crops had been diverted to the building project. Because of the food shortage, some were forced to mortgage properties to buy grain. Despite the famine, the farmers still had to pay exorbitant Persian taxes, and many had to borrow the money by handing over their lands as pledges for repayment. To make matters worse, Jewish creditors, who were unsympathetic to the building project, exploited the builders by demanding payment, tragically forcing some Jews to sell their children into slavery to pay their debts because their lands had been confiscated.

In chapter 5 of his memoir, Nehemiah says: "I was very angry when I heard their protest and these complaints. After thinking it over, I brought charges against the officials and the officers. I told them, 'You are all taking interest from your own people!'" (vv. 6–7). Nehemiah responded to this urgent problem by calling an assembly to remedy the malpractice, and he also limited his own use of tax funds, thereby serving as a model.

The Jews begged Nehemiah to see the situation the way they saw it. Their children were being sold into slavery, and faithful working parents were powerless to prevent it. Although Nehemiah had the authority to enforce regulations as he saw fit, he did not force the creditors with the strong arm of the law. Instead, he appealed to them from a communal point of view and emphasized the term "kin" (5:8). With a large group of the community present, no doubt including some friends and relatives of the wronged parties, Nehemiah pointed out that these creditors were selling "kin" into debt slavery. The community had already withstood external persecution, and now Nehemiah was certainly not going to tolerate oppression from within.

However, there will be obstacles that seem to constantly occur that make it hard to see ongoing progress. To his credit, Nehemiah began to correct the treatment of the builders by his own example. Many of those who had been sold as slaves had been bought back by Nehemiah personally. Although he bore the authority of the king, Nehemiah operated more like the patriarch of a family than a Persian ruler. In contrast to his dealings with external adversaries, he sought genuine agreement from the community, even from those he would need to confront. To this end, he led by example. He not only bought back enslaved members of the community and worked to cancel debts of faithful workers, he also refused the governor's food allowance. In contrast to his less benevolent predecessors, Nehemiah focused his resources on the benefit of the community.

Even when legitimate concerns arise, they can lead to infighting among persecuted people, who initially came together with the best intentions of working for justice. A young activist once shared with me her experience with internal opposition: "I was expecting a little pushback from the outside, but it was the people on the inside that I didn't expect to be the ones who would disagree with me—especially since we were trying to push for something together. That has been the hardest resistance that I've faced. It's with people who totally agree with me—we want the same thing—but we can't get on the same page about how that should occur or if we're doing it the right way and for the right reasons. Everybody's got an opinion and thinks we should do it their way." Most community organizers do not expect to have disagreements with people on their side—those who share a common commitment to justice. This can create infighting in circumstances where people place themselves above critique.

This quandary is summarized well by the editors of *The IVP Women's Bible Commentary*:

> There is always the temptation for oppressed groups or persons to assume an irreproachable hermeneutic stance.

People can deceive themselves into thinking that because they are oppressed, they are beyond critique and that their interpretive stance is correct. By including a unit on internal opposition, the book of Nehemiah draws even the oppressed under the eyes of God's presence. The law of Moses does not differentiate between injustice of oppressors or the oppressed. All are capable and culpable.[4]

After Nehemiah had quelled the infighting within the community, the wall surrounded the city, and the only gaps in the wall were the gateways where the doors needed to be hung. Completion was imminent. Nehemiah's adversaries tried to increase their pressure by luring him away from the work into an unsecured location. The proposed meeting place was the Valley of Ono, seven miles southeast of Joppa. He declined, saying that he was doing a "great" work and he could not leave it to come to their meeting. Nehemiah's enemies, however, would not take no for an answer but persisted, trying four times to set up the meeting. Both the location and the urgency of the matter must have caused Nehemiah to be suspicious about their motives.

When it became clear that they could not lure Nehemiah outside of the city, they bribed a priest named Shemaiah to convince Nehemiah to hide inside the temple so he could avoid danger. The idea of hiding within the temple seems attractive on one level, because no one except an officiating priest could look inside to find him. But as a non-priest, Nehemiah was not allowed by law to enter the sanctuary. Shemaiah's unlawful suggestion was the telltale sign that God had not sent him. Nehemiah came to this priest expecting godly advice but sensed that something was wrong: "I realized that God hadn't sent him at all but that he spoke this prophecy against me because Tobiah and Sanballat had hired him. He was hired to frighten me and to make me sin by acting in this way. Then they could give me a bad name and discredit me" (6:12–13). This was an attempt to terrorize Nehemiah into shutting himself away to neutralize his work. However, he refused to run away and hide in the supposed safety of the temple. Nehemiah used wisdom and discernment to avoid this trap.

The importance of identifying internal opposition underlines the need for self-reflection, especially in any justice-oriented reparation process. We are being enlisted by God to fight poverty, racial discrimination, gender inequity, economic exploitation, and many other rampant forms of injustice. We might be called on to face giants such as gentrification, substandard and unaffordable housing, employment discrimination, child abuse and neglect, gun violence, malnutrition, food deserts, substance abuse, and environmental inequity. Considering these seemingly insurmountable obstacles, we will constantly be faced with the internal opposition of fear. Fear is one of the primary dynamics that comes along with doing the work of God.

This reminds me of a young white pastor who wanted to discuss a challenge he was facing in the multiracial church he planted. He described how an African American brother, who had come alongside to help him build the church, was sexually harassing women and causing great harm in the congregation. As we talked, I learned more about why he found it hard to discipline or ask this man to leave the church. Although he knew what he needed to do, he was frozen by fear. This sincere, young, white pastor came from an affluent white megachurch in the suburbs. He was acutely aware that building a multicultural church is extremely hard to do. It was essential for him to be embraced and found credible by Black and Brown people in the city. Deep inside he feared that, as a white man, he could not do this work without an African American counterpart.

One day I asked him, "If this were a white guy doing this type of harmful behavior toward women at your former church, what would you have done?" He immediately said he would hold him accountable and ask him to step down from ministry. Then I asked, "So why are you not doing that with this Black young man?" He realized how the spirit of fear had caused him to neglect his pastoral duties to protect the people in his church. Even though he remained committed to learning from, partnering with, and submitting to leaders of color, he knew that he had to face his fears and confront this brother, although he might be viewed as a white man unable to share authority with a person of color. This was not true, but he came to see that more important than his reputation was the safety and well-being of women in the church.

We all have fears and can feel frozen by them. We can't just muscle our way forward into courage. In fact, to have courage we must be able to know and acknowledge our fears. To do this, we need help and support that gives us the ability to face our fears and, therefore, not compromise our courage. For most people, this is best done in counseling with a trained therapist. In this safe and trusted environment we are allowed the space to get grounded in the truth. Every young leader has different fears. *What is your unique core fear?*

As a young civil rights leader, Martin Luther King Jr. had to reckon with a core fear. King found strength in what is now known as the "kitchen table prayer." King was dozing off in his bedroom around midnight when the phone rang. "N——, we're tired of your mess," a caller hissed. "And if you aren't out of this town in three days, we're going to blow up your house and blow your brains out." King hung up and walked to his kitchen to heat a pot of coffee. He had been receiving death threats for weeks, ever since he had accepted a request to lead a bus boycott in Montgomery, Alabama. But King was starting to doubt his decision.

As the threats poured in, his fears increased for his wife, Coretta, and their infant daughter, Yolanda. He wondered how he could relinquish his role as the boycott leader without appearing to be a coward. Then something happened that King would talk about for years afterward. He bowed over his untouched cup of coffee and prayed aloud in desperation. King said he heard an "inner voice" that addressed him by name and encouraged him to stand up for justice. That experience reminded King that he could not depend on the resources of his talents and intellectual training to make it in the struggle. He came to see more clearly that spirituality had to be real to him in a special way as he confronted the pressures of the movement. After the kitchen experience, King felt a special divine companionship, what he called "cosmic companionship," that sustained him. Fear left him and he was assured that if he continued to stand up for justice and righteousness, God would be with him.[5]

The call of God to do something significant and the experience of having fear go hand in hand. Expect it. If we're not scared, it probably means we don't understand the magnitude of what we've been called to do. Anything worth doing is going to be scary!

A powerful way to combat fear is to keep the vision in front of you. To cope with fear, remember that you are called to do something good that will help rebuild a community. You're there because you have a vision of how this community could thrive and be revitalized. You see how kids could thrive in a safe space, youth could be trained and mentored, senior citizens could have a place to belong, and people who are hungry could be fed, all with dignity and respect. Remember that you believe in the vision and are willing to work hard to make it a reality.

It is hard enough to do what God has commanded us to do, but it becomes even more difficult when we have to grapple with the resultant opposition. In my experience, many young leaders jump into organizing with idealistic beliefs surrounding the excitement of being involved in the struggle. Consequently, they are often blindsided by the realities of working with actual people. Organizing takes selflessness, because ultimately this work is not about us—it is about the people we are fighting for.

People who step into organizing only because they want to advance their own interests or notability will cause conflict in the group, because that is not a sufficient motivation to do this work. We must recognize that, as with any mission-driven cause, we are working with people who have a personal interest in these issues. People invest their own passions, identities, and traumas in this work, and they bring their own experiences, which differ from our own. Like Nehemiah, we must stay resilient despite the opposition we face, recognizing that we can achieve our end goal only by working together to oppose and settle both external and internal conflicts. The story of Nehemiah suggests that those who do persist, even in the face of fear and intimidation, will succeed. The wall is completed.

SEVEN

Stay Covered in Prayer

So the wall was finished on the twenty-fifth day of the month of Elul. It took fifty-two days. When our enemies heard about this, all of the nations around us were afraid and their confidence was greatly shaken. They knew that this work was completed with the help of our God.

—Nehemiah 6:15–16

In my early days as a preacher, I learned a life lesson that I still live by today. I was invited to preach for a special afternoon service at a large Black Methodist church in Los Angeles, California. I asked one of my former students, who also played the saxophone, to accompany me. We were well received by the congregation as I preached, and he ministered through special music. At the end of my sermon, I invited anyone who needed prayer to come forward. As I waited and surveyed the audience, I saw a woman seated at the end of a pew toward the middle of the church who seemed to be glaring at me. The menacing appearance on her face made me think there was something spiritually wrong, so I decided to go pray for her.

I walked out of the pulpit, went to her seat, placed my hand on her shoulder, and began to pray. Suddenly, she started flailing her arms wildly in the air. At first, I thought she was moved by the Spirit, but she was actually punching me. I could not restrain her, so I looked over my shoulder. The young man who accompanied me saw my distress and immediately came to my rescue, putting his body between us and holding her arms until she calmed down. Eventually, she composed herself.

On our drive home, my young friend and I debriefed the situation, and I realized that as the guest preacher, I felt responsible for taking spiritual authority over what was happening in that church service. However, the truth is, God did not lead me to go and pray for that lady. Instead, it was my own spiritual immaturity that led me to make that costly and embarrassing mistake.

After I got home, I journaled about the incident, and I heard these words rise in my soul: "Don't grow beyond your prayer cover." As I sat with those words, an image came to mind that I had not thought about in years. When my brothers and I were kids, we used to watch a weekly television program called *Combat!* The show focused on the squad leader, Sergeant Chip Saunders, who would often take his platoon into enemy territory. As their leader, Sgt. Saunders would go first. While he was advancing toward danger, he would yell over his shoulder to the soldiers behind him, saying, "Cover me!" Immediately, they would all begin shooting a barrage of bullets in the enemy's direction, allowing Sgt. Saunders to move closer to the enemy and outmaneuver them.

I realized after that incident in church that anyone laboring for the Lord needs covering like that given to Sgt. Saunders. The message was: *You need people who will cover you in prayer. Not like a roof or an umbrella that covers someone's head in inclement weather, but you need people who will protect you in prayer as you advance toward the enemy.* We cannot do the work of reconciliation without having adequate prayer cover. To this day, I have a prayer team that consists of people who have known me for years and are called to the ministry of intercessory prayer. I truly believe that every time we pursue the work of reconciliation, we are like Sgt. Saunders advancing against the enemy, going up against powers and principalities that want to thwart our efforts. We must make sure that we have enlisted people who will cover us with targeted and specific prayer as we advance the ministry of reconciliation.

Nehemiah understood the power of prayer, because the first thing he did in this rebuilding process was pray. In fact, he prayed for fifty-two days, from the beginning to the end of the process (as noted in Neh. 1:4; 4:4, 9; 5:19; 6:9, 14; 13:14, 22, 29, 31). Nehemiah did not seek to act beyond his prayer cover. He constantly sought God for strength, courage, and wisdom, which was evidenced throughout the course of his leadership.

When opposition arose, Nehemiah ignored the scoffers and turned to God for help. It was Yahweh's work that was under attack, so Nehemiah called on the power of God to defend it. He was determined that the workers would not be deterred from completing this important work. Nehemiah prayed and asked God to turn his adversaries into the victims of this conflict. Instead of using political clout against the enemies of this effort, Nehemiah prayed that their evil deeds would be punished by exile as God had previously done to Israel. Confidence shriveled and spirits fell when their enemies and neighbors realized that Nehemiah was supported by supernatural power. Sanballat, one of Nehemiah's primary opponents, tried to disrupt the project, but his efforts only brought more glory to their work. Nehemiah gave credit to God and declared that their neighbors, both friend and foe, had also acknowledged Yahweh's hand in their success.

With the wall completed, he encouraged the people to remember their "great and awesome" God (1:5) and to fix their eyes on him. Nehemiah not only was focused on the building project; he also knew that it was just the start of what God wanted to do. Nehemiah understood that victory was won by a combination of faith in God and practical strategy. Therefore, when they finished the work, the accomplishment was not just the wall; the more profound success was accomplished in the people. What needed to be fixed was larger than just the physical repair of the wall. It was more than the physical reality that was broken. The people were also broken: their hope was broken, their self-esteem was broken, their dreams for themselves and their children were broken, and their sense of safety had been destroyed. The real work was to bring the people together to become a spiritually vibrant and compassionate community.

Spirituality and Activism Go Together

Sadly, sometimes our activism is devoid of spirituality; at other times, our spirituality is devoid of activism. There can be a great gulf between people who think of themselves as spiritual and those who are called to actively engage in this work. However, the global, social, political, and cultural issues that we are facing require us to be both active and spiritually grounded. It can be hard to lean into God when fighting for justice in spaces where the idea of God is being weaponized against us. As a result, people may begin to feel that they cannot turn to God for support and that they must draw on their own strength to fight these battles. However, we know that our own strength is insufficient. We need God, but we must be careful.

When we attempt to bridge spirituality and activism, we must always remember that many people who are involved in social activism have experienced Christianity in negative ways. The very thing that you believe will help someone has often hurt them. An example of this can be seen in activism centered on the inclusion and rights of the LGBTQ+ community. Many LGBTQ+ people have been harmed by the church, and so they may not need you to show up for them through prayer. They may need you to show up for them through your actions, by standing alongside them in protests and walking with them in parades, by speaking up even when it seems unpopular. When the work feels unsustainable, it is important that all of those working toward reconciliation remain rooted in God, recognizing that our outer works come from our inner strength and spiritual grounding.

How easy it is to fall into the trap of focusing on our current or urgent circumstances rather than trusting God. The first thing we must do as we enter reconciliation work is to seek direction and empowerment from God. The fight is ultimately a battle against evil, which at its core is hatred, greed, fear, and divisiveness. Those who oppose reconciliation dehumanize and deny the image of God in people—this sin must be confronted with spiritual strength. Catholic priest and scholar Robert Schreiter explains, "Reconciliation is first a spirituality, not a strategy. God initiates it. Ultimately, reconciliation is not a human achievement, but the work of God within us."[1] When we pray, we admit, *God, I know this is not about how hard I work but about your power to repair broken systems and to heal our communities.*

The book of Nehemiah demonstrates that prayer is how we prepare people to repair the broken systems in their local communities. This powerful spiritual resource can help us find the faith and courage to tackle what appears to be an impossible task. I am an avid activist for prayer to be included as a major part of any process of reconciliation or reparations happening in the places where we live.

This conviction about prayer deepened in me when I was a campus staff member with InterVarsity Christian Fellowship. As someone from a Pentecostal tradition, I was nurtured in a passionate prayer style where people poured their hearts out to God. I still believe in and practice this form of prayer. But I've also come to understand that prayer is not a monologue; it is a dialogue with God. Prayer is a dynamic, interactive process through which we speak to God and God speaks to us, which requires stillness in us.

This idea was beautifully explained by Maggie Gobran, a spiritual and contemplative woman I had the honor to meet at the Global Leadership Summit in Cape Town, South Africa. Everyone called her Mama Maggie. During her keynote address, she said, "Silence your body to listen to your words. Silence your tongue to listen to your thoughts. Silence your thoughts to listen to your heart. Silence the beating of your heart to listen to your spirit. Silence your spirit to listen to his Spirit." Her words continue to speak truth to me, and in InterVarsity this practice is called "listening prayer."

This attentive prayer method is usually done in pairs or small groups, which includes a person leading prayer. Someone in the group may ask to receive prayer, and the others begin listening to the Spirit. When starting with attentive prayer, we determine the true need we are praying for. Although the person receiving prayer has probably asked for something specific, it is important to listen together for God's guidance with our spiritual and natural senses. This might include asking questions to help us better understand the real need.

Once we have a clear sense of direction, we must decide the best way to pray for the concern or situation. One particularly effective approach is to sit quietly and use breath prayers as God brings peace and calm to the person we are praying for. A breath prayer is a form of prayer that combines deep breathing with prayers of meditation taken from God's Word to help calm the body and focus the heart and mind. An example of a breath prayer adapted from Psalm 23 would be to say "I will not be afraid" as you inhale, and "for you are with me" as you exhale. Another example adapted from 1 John is to inhale with "there is no fear" and exhale with "in your love." Invite the Holy Spirit to guide and direct you by bringing any words, Scriptures, or images to mind that would address the need at hand. Pray for discernment, knowing that it is all right to ask questions of God and the person while you pray. Check occasionally to ask how they feel or if they are sensing any impressions or recalling any memories that might be helpful in the prayer process.

Continue to pray as you listen and look for signs of God at work. When the time comes to close, give the person a few suggestions for how they might continue moving forward based on what surfaced in prayer. Even if there were no big insights, end with confidence, knowing that the worst thing that happened is that you genuinely cared for someone in prayer.

Prayer as Solidarity

Prayer can also generate solidarity between people from different life experiences and ethnic backgrounds, especially when praying in response to an injustice. After the senseless murder of a young unarmed Black man, a leader with Inter-Varsity posted this public prayer on Facebook:

> This week the African American and African Diaspora community has experienced deep pain as the story of Ahmaud Arbery's shooting has gone viral. His death resonates with historic acts of violence and injustice that reach back 400 years. Their pain is compounded by the way Covid deaths have disproportionately occurred in the African American community, which reflects decades of intentional under-investment in their neighborhoods, health, and economic well-being. . . .
>
> Lord, we cry out.
>
> With our African American and African Diaspora sisters and brothers, we cry out, "How long, O Lord?"
>
> We cry out with the millions of families that have lost loved ones—beginning with the slave trade to the present moment.
>
> We cry out with churches burying a dozen or more of their senior saints because of Covid-19.
>
> We cry out with mothers and fathers who worry for their children's safety every time they go out.
>
> We cry out for every Black Christian who wonders if they can bear this pain any longer.
>
> We cry out, "Come, Lord Jesus, and bring your kingdom of grace and justice in its fullness."

I cry out, as a Chinese American, to ask your forgiveness for the ways that my community all too often shares in the racialized prejudices that bring pain and suffering to the Black community, even as we experience racialized prejudice ourselves.

We cry out: Lord, have mercy. Lord, reveal your holiness and justice through us.

Lord, have mercy.[2]

This kind of honest confession and deep solidarity with others in prayer can lead people to shift their focus, enabling a new sense of protection and identity to emerge in times of great despair and upheaval.

Nehemiah called the people in Jerusalem to put their focus back on God. Nehemiah began by appointing the Levites and musicians to lead the people in fasting, repentance, and confession. As the people listened to the words of the law, they wept because they recognized that they had violated it many times. A deep awareness of their national sin was brought to their remembrance, and the people were overcome with regret and sorrow. The people agreed with God about what got them into this horrible situation in the first place.

Corporate confession is an acknowledgment of our collective need for God. I did not grow up in a tradition where confession was regularly practiced, but at Quest Church, where I now serve on the pastoral staff, we participate in a weekly rhythm of corporate confession before we take Communion. I have found the practice to be a humbling reminder of the reality that I am not a perfect person, and we are not perfect people. In our fast-paced world that keeps us from taking inventory of ourselves, it can be easy to assume that all is well with our souls. The act of confession reaffirms that we need God's presence in our lives. At Quest Church, this is the confession that we recite as a congregation every week:

> Most merciful God, we confess that we have sinned against you in thought, word and deed, by what we have done and by what we have left undone.
>
> We have not loved you with our whole heart; we have not loved our neighbors as ourselves. Too often we forget to love ourselves as you have first loved us; too often we turn away from pain and injustice, instead of rebuking the powers of this world as you gave us the authority to do.
>
> We are truly sorry and we humbly repent. In the power of Jesus's name, root out and bind all evil, sin, and death, both in our own lives and in our common, connected body, as we remember that we belong to you and to each other.
>
> Forgive us; restore in us the joy of our salvation; renew in us a right spirit that we may delight in your will and walk in your ways, to the glory of Jesus's name. Amen.

This type of confession forces us to face the truth of our humanity. But the prayer of confession is not intended to keep us in guilt and shame; it gives us a chance to agree with God and recommit ourselves to a renewed life through obedience. The people of Jerusalem faced the truth and made an agreement to do things God's way by promising not to trust in idols or themselves anymore. These contrite people realized that only God could make them great, and they were determined to no longer turn to other kings or gods to make a name for themselves.

After they confessed their sins, Nehemiah reminded them, "This day is holy to the LORD your God. Don't mourn or weep" (8:9). He reminded them that it was a day of thanksgiving to God for the new mercies that had been provided.

This was a call to joy. The people's joy was to be based on their confidence that the Lord would protect them. Their gladness in God was proportionate to their faith in God to protect them from and defeat their adversaries. Nehemiah reminded the people of Jerusalem, "The joy from the LORD is your strength" (8:10). He encourages those in Jerusalem that rejoicing in God will give them strength in body, mind, and spirit. This renewal is essential to the physically exhausting and spiritually draining work of reconciliation.

Without intentionally pursuing and engaging in joy, we become overwhelmed by the dejection of the mind and excessive grief, which weakens our spirit and body, making us easy prey for our enemies. This has been scientifically proven to be true. In a *Time* magazine article titled "The Biology of Joy," Michael Lemonick discusses how a group of researchers discovered that having a "happy brain" and possessing hope, optimism, and contentment "appear to reduce the risk or limit the severity of cardiovascular disease, pulmonary disease, diabetes, hypertension, colds, and upper-respiratory infections as well. According to a Dutch study of elderly patients . . . , those upbeat mental states reduced an individual's risk of death 50 percent over the study's nine-year duration."[3]

This study suggests that the joy of the Lord is needed now more than ever. We are living in a sociopolitical climate that carries an ominous sense of threat in the atmosphere. Parents fear for the safety and fair treatment of their children in educational, social, judicial, financial, political, and medical systems. Hard-won progress is being challenged and reversed. Continued legislative efforts jeopardize the access to health care for millions of Americans and their children, especially those with chronic or preexisting conditions. These harsh realities have caused people to feel despondent and to lose hope. The ability to feel joy has been compromised by social realities, which is why people who are committed to justice must be not only active in fixing these injustices but also committed to praying for the restoration of joy.

Steve Hayner, a person I worked with many years ago, was known for his joy. He became the president of InterVarsity Christian Fellowship in 1988, near the end of an unstable and difficult decade in which InterVarsity had five presidents. He brought healing and hope to a community that had undergone so much uncertainty and trauma. He died of pancreatic cancer at just sixty-six years old and learned a lot about the importance of joy in the process. In a conversation with a dear friend before his death, he said, "Life is a whole lot less complicated and a whole lot more joyful than I'd ever imagined. The grace and love of God permeate more of life than we dare realize. Often, I've taken life and myself way too seriously, and God never meant life to be lived that way. It's meant to be lived with joy and playfulness. The outcome is good and terrific. I wish I'd played more. But now I'll have lots of opportunity to grow into that."[4] As C. S. Lewis says, "Joy is the serious business of Heaven."[5]

For both Steve and me, one of our greatest joys has been working with young adults. Over the years, I have come to believe that God is birthing something new in the coming generations. I am adamant that the coming generation remain grounded in prayer given the challenges before them and the resistance they will face as they confront broken systems. The current sociopolitical climate is evil. The legislative decisions have the potential to destroy people's lives and limit their capacity to thrive. Like Nehemiah, this generation must pray and seek God's guidance before taking the first step. Prayer must be a constant practice throughout the journey. We can never forgo our spiritual cover. We must pray to build solidarity and unity among people. We must pray and encourage others to confess their participation in unjust systems. We must pray and seek the joy of the Lord to build our strength so that we can continue when things get hard and when obstacles seem insurmountable. With this in mind, I commend this prayer to you as you seek to make this vision a reality:

> Grant us, Lord God, a vision of your world as your love would have it: a world where the weak are protected, and none go hungry or poor; a world where the riches of creation are shared so everyone might enjoy them; a world where different races, cultures, and creeds live in peace and harmony, with equal regard; a world where peace is built with justice, and justice is guided by love. Give us the inspiration and courage to go forth with willing hearts, minds, and bodies to build such a world, through Christ Jesus. Amen.[6]

EIGHT

Avoid Faithful Exhaustion

I wasn't in Jerusalem while this was happening because I had gone to Babylon's King Artaxerxes in the thirty-second year of the king. After some time, I asked the king's permission and returned to Jerusalem.

—Nehemiah 13:6–7

After the fall of apartheid, South Africa instituted the Truth and Reconciliation Commission, led by Archbishop Desmond Tutu. The commission operated for seven difficult years with a purpose to promote reconciliation, healing, and closure for perpetrators and victims of apartheid. In the second year of this painful tribunal, in 1997, Bishop Tutu publicly revealed that he had prostate cancer. He wrote, "[Cancer] probably would have happened whatever I had been doing. But it seemed to demonstrate that we were engaging in something costly. Forgiveness and reconciliation were not to be entered into lightly, facilely. My illness seemed to dramatize the fact that it is a costly business to try to heal a wounded and traumatized people and that those engaging in this crucial task may bear the brunt themselves. It may be that we have been a great deal more like vacuum cleaners than dishwashers, taking into ourselves far more than we knew of the pain and devastation of those whose stories we had heard."[1]

Tutu's image of the work of reconciliation being internalized in us, like a vacuum cleaner instead of a dishwasher, shook me to the core. The thought that all the hurt, pain, anger, and trauma we hear and hold for others while working for reconciliation may lodge itself inside us was deeply alarming. I became convinced that self-care is not a luxury but a necessity for those engaged in this costly work.

The work of restoration was certainly costly for Nehemiah. He had taken on the pain and suffering of the Jews during their lengthy rebuilding process. Reinforcing the gaps and repairing the wall required fifty-two days of hard work. The complete rebuild of the walls of Jerusalem took about four years. Nehemiah served as governor of Jerusalem for a total of twelve years. After the wall was built, it was necessary that this influential leader take a leave of absence. By this point, he was emotionally, physically, and mentally exhausted. Nehemiah needed a break!

Not only was Nehemiah in need of respite, it was culturally appropriate for him to do so as well. It was customary in the ancient Near East for kings to require their servants to physically return to reaffirm their allegiance. Nehemiah was still a servant of King Artexerxes during his time in Jerusalem, so it was only right for him to return to Persia, where he remained for one year. He chose an ideal time to leave

Jerusalem because there were signs of normal life returning to the once-destitute city. Spiritual and ethical leadership was reestablished, the wall was dedicated, worship was restored, and people returned to Jerusalem, which was now a place of growth and development. With the hard work behind him, Nehemiah continued teaching the people by demonstrating the importance of taking time to rejuvenate.

Respite is essential to regain strength to continue the work. If we aren't careful, we can become so absorbed in our good work that we forget the necessity of rest. I was reminded of this unexpectedly at a prayer meeting one Sunday morning after worship service. I prayed with a young white woman who was sitting next to me. I appreciated her spiritual sensitivity and thoughtfulness as she prayed. When we finished, I told her that I was glad she had joined us. Then she said that she'd heard something in prayer for me and asked if she could share it. I agreed. She looked at me and said two words: "Faithful exhaustion."

She continued by saying that I work hard and need rest. I started to respond, but before I could say anything, she looked at me and said, "Rest." She recognized that my exhaustion came as a result of being faithful. It was as if she was saying that only rest could address my level of exhaustion. I felt stunned as I left that prayer meeting because I'd never heard the words "faithful" and "exhaustion" used together. I agreed that she had heard from God on my behalf. I was working myself to exhaustion, trying to demonstrate my faithfulness to God, to my students, to my church, and to the leaders I mentor, which was not sustainable. I needed rest.

Confronting gender bias and ethnic discrimination, racism, and hate crimes is exhausting—and doing so can cause mental and emotional injuries to those doing the work. Any person who has suffered an emotionally painful, sudden, or uncontrollable racist encounter is at risk of having a race-based traumatic stress injury. In the United States, Black, Indigenous, and people of color are most vulnerable due to living under extreme psychological and emotional distress within a system of white supremacy. In his book *My Grandmother's Hands: Racialized Trauma and the Pathway to Mending Our Hearts and Bodies*, Resmaa Menakem, an anti-racist educator, writes, "For most Americans, including most of us with dark skin, white-body supremacy has become a part of our bodies. How could it not? It's the equivalent of a toxic chemical we ingest on a daily basis. Eventually, it changes our brains and the chemistry of our bodies."[2]

I experienced that kind of pain after the police officers who shot and killed Breonna Taylor were not indicted on any charges related to her death. Sadly, news of the lack of indictment came sixty-five years to the day when the white racist men who brutally killed Emmett Till were acquitted. Now the police who killed Taylor, a young woman, while she was asleep in her bed were not indicted. I knew the system was built this way, and it was working exactly as intended, but hearing the news was still unbearably painful. I needed a place to restore my soul.

This was deeply personal to me as a Black woman. Breonna Taylor was just one year older than my daughter. She had hopes and dreams like any other young woman. Taylor had once said, "I want to be the one who finally breaks the cycle of my family's educational history. I want to be the one to finally make a difference. I want to be the one that everybody can look up to with smiles on their faces, telling me how proud of me they are."[3] Instead, people were marching in the streets of this country demanding justice as her dreams were buried along with her body. I was tired and needed a place to grieve, reflect, and renew my soul.

Although it was during the Covid pandemic and few churches were meeting indoors, I found an outdoor, meditative space that had been created for prayer and reflection. It was at a church in South Seattle, and the online invitation was exactly what I needed: "Come grieve, reflect, learn, pray, and hope for racial justice at stations set up in Rainier Avenue Church's parking lot. . . . We hope this space will be a refuge and an encouragement to you!"[4] A friend and I attended together. As we silently walked through this meditative space, I could feel the tension in my body begin to unravel. It was restorative just to be in a quiet place with others as I slowly walked in silence breathing, thinking, and praying. I needed to be restored so that I could carry on with my reconciliation work.

The pain of living within the American racialized social construct affects not just Black people. Everybody, regardless of their racial or ethnic background, faces some degree of trauma living in a racialized society. Menakem says, "While white-body supremacy benefits white Americans in some ways, it also does great harm to white bodies, hearts and psyches."[5] The body is where our instincts reside, where we fight, flee, or freeze as we endure the trauma inflicted by the racial and social ills that plague us. Reconcilers must understand the importance of caring for their bodies and the bodies of others to facilitate the healing needed from living in a racialized society.

Audre Lorde, the renowned Black writer, feminist, womanist, and civil rights activist, suggests that self-care is an act of radical political engagement: "Caring for myself is not self-indulgence, it is self-preservation, and that is an act of political warfare."[6] Self-care is a radical act because people working for change don't feel like they have time to take care of themselves amid the pressing demands of the movement. This is particularly true for Black women, who have histori-cally been expected to take care of everybody else. Taking care of myself is an important and radical act of defiance, because it goes against everything that a Black woman has been conditioned to believe.

Define What Your Self-Care Means

Many years ago, I was invited to speak at a women's retreat in Southern California at one of the most opulent hotels I have ever seen. There were even black swans swimming in a pond near the entrance! After checking in, I got into the elevator to go to my room, and there were two young, Latinx women already inside. One asked the other, "Do we belong here?" I overheard their conversation and immediately un-derstood what they meant.

The lavish wealth displayed throughout the establishment made them question whether they fit in at such an extrava-gant place. They wondered whether they were good enough to be there. As I got off the elevator, I realized that I felt the same way. It was as if we, as women of color, believed that restorative beauty and the accompanying respite was only reserved for white people with money. That hotel was no place for those women or me. The truth is, though, as women of color, we were inherently worthy of being there, and we needed to be there because our bodies are always doing the physically, emotionally, and mentally demanding work of justice, whether formally or not. But we felt uncomfortable and doubted our belonging because we rarely receive the permission, nor do we often have the resources, for restoration.

Despite the lack of permission or resources, it is essential for us to decide and define for ourselves what self-care means, with specific actions that we can plan into our schedule. I highly recommend the following baseline recommendations from scholar and organizer Kim Tran:

1. Disengage from social media, but stay engaged in current events.
2. It's okay to be broken. Give yourself time to heal.
3. How accessible are you to media? Consider getting rid of your news app and designate a specific time to engage.
4. Know your boundaries and have a mantra to protect them. For example, "Hey, it's good to see you, and I'm so grateful that you trust me with this story. But I'm kind of at capacity for talking about classism/racism/ableism/patriarchy right now. Would you mind if we switched topics?"
5. Activist guilt is real. Give yourself permission to say no.[7]

Those of us working in reconciliation must learn to give ourselves permission to practice self-care and rest. Understanding our ability to say no is as vital as the marches, teach-ins, and walk-outs that we participate in. As someone who is outgoing, friendly, and eager to please others, I have fallen into the trap of saying yes when I should have said no. Over the years, however, I have grown to understand the importance of setting boundaries for myself. To help remind me of this commitment, I purchased a sweatshirt that says, "She believed she could, but she needed a break, so she said no." I took a picture of myself wearing that shirt and posted it on social media. To my surprise, almost five thousand people reacted positively to that picture! Their response convinced me that the need to establish firm boundaries is true for many others.

Maintaining our boundaries to make space to care for ourselves will look different for everyone. There is no right way to do self-care. However, any form of self-care will require planning and practice, and it will require a deep connection with our body. We can't reconcile with others if we are not reconciled with ourselves. Spiritual director and author Ruth Haley Barton says, "Truly, the best thing any of us have to bring to leadership is our own transforming selves."[8] This will take work, but the growth, healing, and life transformation that result are well worth it. This transformational endeavor benefits not just us but also others who have experienced similar exhaustion as a result of racialized trauma, as well as those who come behind us in this work. Menakem explains: "When you heal a soul wound, you heal the people who came before you. You heal their presence in your life, in your memory, and in the expression of your DNA. This opens up a bit more room for flow and compassion inside you. You also heal the generations to come, because your healing means that you will not pass on your trauma to your descendants."[9]

Start by learning to listen to your body. It will tell you what you need—to rest, to drink water, or to have a good laugh to release stress. We cannot be our best if we operate out of a disconnected self. Some form of physical exercise and caring for our bodies is vital to our ability to accomplish what God has called us to do. Once, while halfway through running a 5K race, I began to get tired and run out of steam. While I was doubting my capacity to finish, I heard a question rise in my spirit: "Do you have the faith to finish this race?" Tired and exhausted, I said, "Yes, Lord." Then I heard these words from God: "I am the author and the finisher of your faith. If you have the faith, I'll finish it." I ran the rest of that race knowing that, if I kept the faith, God would give me the strength to finish. As we continue in this long, hard work of reconciliation, know that the longevity to stay comes from caring for ourselves and trusting God.

Since moving to the Pacific Northwest, I have increasingly discovered nature to be deeply restorative to my body and spirit. I grew up in the city and assumed a false narrative that Black people are not comfortable outdoors. I now know that is not true! Our ancestors, such as Harriet Tubman, were able to navigate their way to freedom because of their intimate knowledge of the outdoors. Sadly, over time, many Black and Brown people lost their connection to the land because they were forced to live in urban "ghettos" due to unfair housing policies, economic bias, and racial discrimination.

This has had an adverse effect on Black and Brown people, especially children, who have little access to nature in urban areas. Instead of experiencing the healing power of nature, they are surrounded by asphalt and concrete and criticized for being so "hard." Could it be that their lack of connection with the beauty of the outdoors has contributed to their tough demeanor? When I'm outside in green space, I notice that my shoulders start to relax and I breathe more deeply. I feel more carefree and there is a lessened sense of urgency, anxiety, and worry. Ideas come to mind. Revelation visits my spirit, and my creativity begins to flow. I can hear the beginning of sermons. Illustrations seem to float to the surface of my soul. Spending time with God in God's creation is an amazing form of self-care and restoration.

Finding Rhythms of Rest

Another powerful self-care practice God gives to us is the practice of a weekly Sabbath. This word literally means to "cease" or "stop." Through the gift of the Sabbath, God's people are called to cease from their labor so they can rest, refresh, and refuel. This reminds us that we were created to be human *beings* and not human *doings*. We are no longer bound to nonstop work rhythms and habits. Instead, Sabbath-keeping is the primary discipline that helps us live within the limits of our humanity and to honor God as our Creator. It is the key to a life lived in sync with the rhythms that God built into our world.

Setting aside a day of rest is difficult, especially in today's remote work environment that causes our work to creep into our homes and families. It is, therefore, vitally important that we intentionally allow this restorative spiritual practice to become a rhythm in our lives. To maintain our physical health and spiritual well-being, we need rest. When we are rested, we deal better with stress and busy schedules. When we take time to refuel spiritually, we're better equipped to deal with challenges and trials that will always be part of our lives. When we sense that God is calling us to take a break, we must submit to the voice of the Good Shepherd, who knows we need to "rest in grassy meadows" and be led to "restful waters" (Ps. 23:2).

How do you care for yourself? What are your rhythms of Sabbath and rest? What practices do you have that help you feel or know that you are in your body and present to yourself? What brings you back into your body? These are the questions you must entertain to create a healthy balance of work and rest that leads to longevity in the demanding ministry of reconciliation.

All my mentors have had longevity in this work. They were not overnight wonders or people who achieved fly-by-night success. They stayed in the game for the long haul. I have observed how their spirituality and ability to pace and care for themselves enabled them to stay actively involved over the long haul. Their longevity is crucial, because the work of reconciliation takes a long time. It is important for us to pace ourselves so we can stay actively committed and equipped to go the distance and complete our assignment.

At this point in the narrative, Nehemiah has done his job. He has helped the people reach a place of stability. Leadership has been established and people have been assigned to keep the workers on task. Now Nehemiah must trust God as he takes this leave of absence. The text doesn't say what he did while he was away. All we know is that he took a significant amount of time away from the rebuilding process. When he left, Nehemiah had to trust that the people would stay the course. Likewise, we must know that the outcome and sustainability of the work depends on God and the people, not on us.

Remember that, while we are working to help rebuild communities, our God is also healing and rebuilding us. Therefore, we must know when to go and when to stop, when to work and when to rest. I believe God will give us the strength to finish what we've been called to do, and when we return we will also be renewed.

NINE

Leverage Access
to Resources

"May the king also issue a letter to Asaph the keeper of
the king's forest, directing him to supply me with timber
for the beams of the temple fortress gates, for the city
wall, and for the house in which I will live."
    The king gave me what I asked, for the gracious power
of my God was with me.

—Nehemiah 2:8

I had originally thought this chapter would fall at the beginning of this book, because the Scripture text is found in the
second chapter of Nehemiah. But after serious thought, I
realized it was critical to first establish the urgent need for
reconciliation and reparations while also enumerating the
unimaginable scope of the work involved before delving into

the subject of resources. I have been actively working as a reconciliation leader for over forty years and can assure you that if you don't have resources, you cannot complete the work. Finances are essential to make the vision of inclusion, justice, and equity a reality. Like Nehemiah, we must face the truth that rebuilding a city or community will require resources. We cannot fully execute a plan for reparations or develop a practice of reconciliation until and unless we wrestle with the wealth gaps (especially racial wealth gaps) in this country.

In this chapter of the biblical text, we see how Nehemiah obtains resources to support his calling to repair the walls of the city of Jerusalem. He uses his cupbearer's access to bring the situation to the attention of one whom he knows has the means to help solve the problem. When Nehemiah learned about the devastation of his people, he allowed the depth of his concern to be visible to the king. A cupbearer's appearance was critical, since he was the one responsible for the king's safety regarding the wine. Any display of discontent on the countenance of Nehemiah would cause great consternation to the king and those around him. In fact, the text says that Nehemiah had never looked sad in the presence of the king before (2:1). The king was both surprised and concerned by Nehemiah's visible anguish. The king shares his concern, and his perceptive words lead Nehemiah to divulge the troublesome matter on his heart.

Nehemiah begins by wisely presenting the matter as a personal issue, referring to the city of Jerusalem as the "graves of his fathers." Nehemiah is smart and strategic in how he presents the problem to the king. He does not mention the city by name. Nehemiah is sensitive to his audience. By keeping his concern general, he allows King Artaxerxes to save face because he was the leader who stopped the work on Jerusalem's restoration years prior, which contributed, at least in part, to the city's current condition.

Nehemiah does not start with a request for the resources. Instead, he initiates his request with a reasonable plea to repair the city where his ancestral graves are located. In the ancient world, the dead were often revered and worshiped and were thought to bring harm to those who did not bury them properly. Nehemiah uses their shared cultural understanding to gain the king's buy-in for the project. Surprisingly, the king doesn't ask questions or seek out details to Nehemiah's request. He only wants to know how long it will take.

Only after the king provides his approval does Nehemiah clearly outline the resources he needs. He asks for official letters to ensure his safe passage on the journey to Jerusalem. He also asks for access to the royal forest. He knows that he will need wood to build a fortress to guard the temple, a city wall, and a residence for himself. The king agrees to all of Nehemiah's requests and even goes further by appointing an armed guard to accompany him.

Proximity to Power

Nehemiah's story does not cast a picture of some fairy tale that simply suggests we can pray our way into renewal. Instead, Nehemiah's story clearly shows that meaningful and lasting repair of our communities will take time and resources. What resources do we bring to this work? We all have some degree of access to power and resources—financial, human resources, social capital, natural resources, and so on. The only question is, How will we leverage them and for whom?

Nehemiah was able to secure resources to support his mission of repair because he had access to the king. He represents a particular social location. He is a man in a man's world. He is a Jew, and because of his job, he has access to a certain degree of power. Nehemiah could walk into the palace in a way that was different from others who did not have the same degree of access to the king and other people in power. Social location and proximity to power affect our ability to access resources. There are some young people who are called to this work who, like Nehemiah, have access to power and resources through their maleness, whiteness, family's social network, educational connections, and so on. These are all forms of currency that are often unrecognized or taken for granted by those who have them.

It is necessary to assess the relational, political, financial, social, cultural, and spiritual networks to which you are connected. You must be able to identify the people who represent King Artaxerxes in your life. I encourage you to take a moment to examine your level of access by reflecting on the following questions:

- What is your social location?
- What connections do you have with those in power?
- What levels of access do you have?

It is important for those who operate in spaces of privilege and who hold greater access to resources to acknowledge it and humbly seek to leverage this access for the greater good.

We must acknowledge that certain bodies can get into places, sit at tables, and converse with influencers that others cannot. For instance, a white person may have access to places of privilege and power that are primarily reserved for whiteness. They can use this access to help other white people discuss and hopefully disavow their mistaken belief in the zero-sum paradigm that causes them to think certain people are worthy of being on top and other people on bottom. White people must honestly admit that this is their problem to solve because they created it. Therefore, when discussing what needs to be repaired, those who are white must acknowledge that whiteness and racial inequality, based on white supremacy, must be addressed. While helping to confront brokenness in communities, white people must repair the destructive nature of whiteness, understanding that they are the only ones who can dismantle it. People from European American backgrounds who are committed to reconciliation must have hard conversations with each other to name where the tensions exist and to own their complicity with creating systems of sustained harm for communities of color.

For example, a young journalist named Steffi Cao was on National Public Radio discussing a topic called the "Vanilla Girl" trend. During the interview, she explained that white women have politically fallen out of favor over the past few years and have been labeled "Karens" as a pejorative term to describe middle-class white women who use their privilege to demand their own way. The use of such privilege follows a long and troubling legacy of white women in the United States weaponizing their victimhood. In her book, *The Sum of Us*, Heather McGhee unpacks the origins of this behavior: "Racial hierarchy offered white people a reprieve from the class hierarchy and gave white women an escape valve from gender oppression. White women in slaveholding communities considered their slaves 'their freedom,' liberating them from farming, housework, child rearing, nursing, and even the sexual demands of their husbands."[1] This legacy gave white women the political currency of being treated like the perfect victim while also perpetuating white supremacy.

As a Black, female reconciliation leader, I have seen this posture subvert white women's ability to submit to the leadership of women of color. This sense of entitlement and posture as the "perfect victim," instead of fostering allyship, causes competition for empathy and attention by overidentification with Black and Brown people, which requires people of color to validate the pain of white women, often leaving little emotional or spiritual resources to acknowledge their own trauma and suffering. This impedes and severely undermines the urgent work of reconciliation. This is not to say that all white women or people are the same. But it is true that whiteness gives a certain privilege in the United States and around the world. Working to dismantle this false identity can lead to conversations about reparations that would not only help restore the lives of people and communities harmed by whiteness but also heal the descendants of those who created it.

Racial injustice may impact certain people directly, but in truth, it hurts everyone. The Chinese American philosopher and activist Grace Lee Boggs once said in an interview with Bill Moyers: "I don't expect moral arguments to take hold with the powers-that-be. They are in their positions of power. They are part of the system. They are part of the problem. . . . I think we're not looking sufficiently at what is happening at the grassroots in the country. We have not emphasized sufficiently the cultural revolution that we have to make among ourselves in order to force the government to do differently. Things do not start with governments."[2]

Those called to reconciliation must wrestle with how to leverage their access to privilege and power while respecting the wisdom and experience of others. Using influence and access responsibly starts by knowing that people have various degrees of proximity to decision-makers and resources. For example, people who are engaged on the front lines, who provide direct services to those who are hurting in communities of need, may have less access to the materials needed to complete that work. Conversely, those furthest from the fight may have material means but lack the lived experience to effectively develop viable solutions to address the racial and social injustices plaguing our society. Unless the resources meet those who understand how to make an impact, the problems will persist.

There are people of color who are leveraging their access to and credibility with those who live in under-resourced communities to help them fight for quality education for their children, gun safety in their neighborhoods, and inclusion in major decision-making processes regarding their lives. Regardless of racial background, resources are needed for these concerned citizens to achieve their goals. I have met amazing people who know the streets, know the harm that is happening to people, and know what is necessary to fix it. They are responding to kids being shot. They know how to support young people. They know that kids need safety in schools, young people need access to jobs, and all people deserve wholesome places of vitality and possibilities to live. They know what works, if only they had the time and resources to implement it!

This is a significant challenge for Nehemiah-type reconcilers, especially those who are on the new journey of awakening. On one hand, they have access to valuable resources, but on the other hand, their understanding about how to appropriately include and respect others is missing. They are sincerely trying to be helpful, but their efforts often fall short. Young Nehemiah leaders must have multiple opportunities to learn from people of various socioeconomic backgrounds and lived experiences to come together and work to repair the brokenness around us.

This reconciling and reparational work must be grounded in integrity by having leaders frequently ask questions, such as:

- Who are we going to learn from and identify with?
- Who will we be in solidarity with?
- What does it mean to leverage access to privilege, influence, and resources?

The answer to these questions will enable us to avoid being a good-hearted person with privilege, who believes we are helping but instead are engaging in toxic charity by creating power imbalances that disrespect a person's dignity or disregard a community's history under the guise of "making an impact."

Respectfully Receiving Feedback

There are young leaders who recognize the need for repair and reparations, and they may have identified what resources to bring to the work, but often they lack the proper instincts to be effective in a culturally respectful manner. Their intentions are pure, but they need feedback from those who may not have the same access to material resources but who have the wisdom of lived experience. A Nehemiah leader, to be successful, will desperately need to listen to folks with life experiences from across the socioeconomic spectrum.

Reconcilers must truthfully face the fact that they are on different journeys from one another and have different starting places as they engage in this work. Unfortunately, I have watched young leaders without this grounding make innocent mistakes that cost them their credibility. Those who are open to hearing this hard-earned wisdom will receive wonderful and transformational truths.

An early cohort of mentees of mine included serious young leaders who were called to reconciliation. They were a group of eight people with women and men, some who grew up in difficult situations and others who represented places of privilege. In one of our large group debriefing sessions, a young white male leader shared that he was thinking about resources and how he was going to pursue them. A few of the leaders, who represented people on the margins, had strong feelings about the way he described his plans. They didn't doubt him and they believed his heart was true, but they were concerned about his methodology. I asked them if they would share their concerns, but they were hesitant because they were not sure he would be willing to hear their feedback. However, out of care for this brother, they eventually shared their concerns. Initially, he was nervous and jumpy, but as he listened, he agreed that he desperately needed to hear their insights. We found that working across the breadth of the socioeconomic spectrum brought great depth to the issues we discussed.

Nehemiah leaders from all backgrounds must understand how to serve as a conduit for resources to reach the need and make a difference. As someone who has mentored many young emerging leaders from working-class and middle-class families, I know the obstacles they face and the insecurities these leaders must wrestle with when raising financial support. It usually requires going into dominant-culture churches or funding organizations to explain the purpose and importance of their ministry. In this process, they will be required to answer questions and justify their request, while walking a fine line between being culturally honest and sharing what they know the funders want to hear. They know what will empower people in their community, but they also know that those with resources will withhold funding if they think the work is too "radical" or "woke."

The reality is that those with the resources decide the terms for funding, and on some level, we must play by their rules. Yet, it is important to be mindful that bowing to the whims or preferences of funders can prevent organizations that seek to do the work of racial restoration and reparations from living fully into their missional integrity. This dilemma can keep leaders from doing the work they are called to do because they are constantly worried about upsetting those who control their access to the finances needed to get the job done.

People of color with lived experience must interrogate the terms on which their work is being funded and have a clear understanding of the motivation of those seeking to extend resources. If a person with financial means censors those who are in proximity to the people doing the work, one must ask what gives others the power or insight to dictate the terms of engagement. I have questioned this when I've been invited to speak and then censored by those who control the purse strings by telling me what I can and can't talk about or address. I have been told, directly and indirectly, not to bring up racism, sexuality, or women in pastoral ministry. When this happens, I realize they have invited my gift but not my full personhood. They have

requested a performance but did not desire a transformational experience. Often, dominant-culture organizations
really want people of color to bring their "flavor" but not
their authenticity.

In 1970, evangelist Tom Skinner gave a prophetic plenary
address at the Urbana Student Missions Conference. His
message became known as "Christ the Liberator." Skinner
called for a radical, just Christianity that set people free
both spiritually and physically. He powerfully spoke into
the climate of protest and activism of that generation of
students, and he was a major catalyst in InterVarsity's racial
reconciliation journey. He said, "There is no possible way
you can talk about preaching the gospel if you do not want
to deal with the issues that bind people. . . . Any gospel that
does not . . . speak to the issue of enslavement, does not
speak to the issue of injustice, does not speak to the issue
of inequality—any gospel that does not want to go where
people are hungry and poverty-stricken and set them free
in the name of Jesus Christ is not the gospel."[3] Regrettably,
after that sermon, most white evangelicals charged Skinner with being too political and stopped inviting him to
speak at their conferences. His weekly radio program was
canceled, and they stopped selling his books. This severely
hurt his vibrant national ministry, and he returned to his
local evangelistic work, speaking in churches and reaching
people in cities.

Although Tom Skinner's message was not received well
by those in power, it was a rally call to my generation, and
that is what I want to give to you. The Nehemiah leader with
any degree of power must listen and learn. It is beneficial
to have access to resources, but if you don't understand
your own identity, racial and social class, and emotional

intelligence, you run the risk of doing more harm than good. I hope you will leverage your access to resources as a collaborative, communal practice to repair broken racial and social structures so all people can reach their full, God-given potential.

Conclusion

Redefine Success

Remember me, my God, concerning this. Don't erase my good deeds that I have done for my God's house and for its services.

—Nehemiah 13:14

I know how it feels to want to throw in the towel. I also know how it feels to wonder if what you did really made a difference. I have questioned whether all the work, energy, and time I had invested was worth it. I have stood in front of a church at the end of a sermon and I have given the final lecture for a class and I have written the last sentence of a book wondering whether my efforts would make any difference.

This is exactly what Nehemiah struggled with. He returned to Jerusalem after a year away, having imagined that everything would be as he left it—the walls restored, the gates rebuilt. Instead, he discovered that the people had relapsed into their former ways of living. The religion of the Jews had deteriorated, while their old enemies, Sanballat and Tobiah, had gained influence in Jerusalem. During Nehemiah's absence, the people of God—even after worship, even after rededicating themselves to God—had fallen back into ruin and sin.

They had broken covenant promises they agreed to at the dedication of the city wall. They had not paid tithes for the support of the temple personnel. And since the Levites had not received their rightful portions of agricultural gifts, they were forced to leave their temple responsibilities and support themselves by farming. Another broken promise was that the people were working and trading on the Sabbath. The Jews had turned what God called holy into a common workday. Nehemiah was furious and responded with immediate action.

Like Nehemiah, we will also have disappointments while engaged in the work of repairing broken communities. There are no guarantees that everything will go the way we planned, and people will not always behave as promised. Folks will disappoint us and we will feel like giving up. That's when it is imperative to entrust the community into the hands of God and pray for the faith and strength to continue the work. Like Nehemiah, we must never forget that this work of repair is ultimately God's work. In his prayer, Nehemiah emphasizes that what he has done was not for political reasons but out of devotion to God's house and its servants, although in the moment it seems like the devotion to his people is misplaced. He asks God to remember him for his actions even when it appears that the people have forgotten. He prays that the work will be credited to him and that his love for his people and faithfulness to God will be recorded. Nehemiah thought his work was finished, but he realized, upon his return, that there was much left to do.

This text is a sober reminder that the work of repair and reconciliation is never complete. I have referred to reconciliation as an ongoing spiritual process. It is not static. We are always in the process of reconciling as we live between the right now and the not yet. The late John Lewis, civil rights activist and congressman, reminds us of this, saying, "Freedom is not a state; it is an act. . . . Freedom is a continuous action we all must take, and each generation must do its part to create an even more fair, more just society."[1] It is my sincere hope that this book will be a useful tool to empower the next generation to be well equipped to have longevity in this work.

I have met many young leaders and activists who are motivated by righteous zeal, passion, and idealism in their attempt to create a more just and inclusive society. However, if the situation does not change in the way they wanted or if people revert to former ways after giving their best efforts, the temptation to give up is strong. To avoid feeling defeated, young leaders must reorient themselves and develop new standards for measuring success. The true measure of success is determined by longevity, resilience, and the ability to continue in the work over the long haul. Adam Grant, organizational psychologist and author of *Think Again*, agrees that it's vital to redefine "success": "Meaning is about making a difference, not having an audience. It's better to be valued by a few than to be known by many. Your contribution is not the scope of your reach. It's the depth of your impact. Your legacy is not how many footprints you leave. It's how long they last."[2]

Longevity is one of the characteristics that distinguishes me as a reconciliation leader, but I didn't plan it this way. It happened one step at a time, following the breadcrumbs on the path that Jesus laid out for me. I was raised in the Black Pentecostal church, and I went to seminary to increase my theological knowledge and sharpen my preaching gifts. During my last year of seminary, I did a practicum at a primarily white college campus and felt compelled to find, include, and minister to students of color in culturally relevant ways. That's how I accidentally stumbled into the ministry of reconciliation. I continued that work for fourteen years and learned many principles and practical strategies along the way. Then a lovely couple with financial resources, who regularly prayed for me and supported my ministry financially, said that God impressed upon them that I should get my doctorate degree and they offered to pay for it. I was stunned but later agreed. It was during my doctoral studies that I developed the Roadmap to Reconciliation model that continues to inform my coaching, consulting, and teaching today.

I am now a professor of reconciliation studies and the associate pastor of preaching and reconciliation at my local church. I certainly have had longevity in this work and hope that I have also had an impact, particularly among the young people who are the next generation of reconciliation leaders, the Nehemiah leaders. In closing, I want to leave you with some important tools to encourage you to stay the course so that your work in repairing broken systems and healing wounded communities will have both longevity and impact.

1. Hold On to Your Hope

I once heard the conductor of an orchestra made up of young Palestinian and Israeli musicians say this about hope: "We don't have the luxury to bathe in pessimism. . . . When we don't believe, we have to make believe."[3] Without hope, we become powerless. But when we feel hopeful, we manage to find the energy to keep going against all odds. Over the course of your journey in this work, it is important to resist becoming frozen by doubt and defeat. The following anonymous quote is pertinent: "Hope has two beautiful daughters; their names are Anger and Courage. Anger at the way things are, and Courage to see that they do not remain as they are." Hope supplies the energy that sustains courage-based action.

2. Keep It Moving

Movement is a medicine for creating change in one's physical, emotional, and mental states. I would call you to maintain your momentum and keep pushing for what you believe. Activist and songwriter Joan Baez is credited with saying, "Action is the antidote to despair." Even if you want to quit, rest if you must, but don't stop. Keep trying. Keep strategizing. Keep organizing. Keep listening. Keep loving. There is an Indigenous proverb that says, "We make the road by walking." Although there may be people who seem to be an overnight success, the truth is the capacity and longevity to remain engaged in this reparational work happens as you stay on the path, taking one faithful step at a time.

3. Don't Go It Alone

You cannot be successful in this journey if you insist on going it alone. It can be hard for young leaders born into a Western, individualistic society to seek help, collaboration, and community, yet you must embrace a collective mindset in order to be successful. It is vitally important that you go together. Reconciliation is only possible when we reject the cultural norm of individualism—that our problems exist in a vacuum, and we are entirely responsible for our own fate—and recognize that we cannot fully understand ourselves apart from each other. When we shift this paradigm, it is evident that our stories and our identities are intertwined, and, therefore, the other's struggles are my own.

After reading what I have written and hopefully understanding the story of Nehemiah better, as well as hearing more of my story, you have become part of my story and I have become part of yours. That's what happens when we come together, work together, pray together, and struggle together to solve problems for the common good. When we intertwine our stories, we are writing a new collective narrative that will help make the world a better place. This will not be easy. As an advocate for African American equality and a leader of the civil rights movement, Coretta Scott King knows about the challenges we face: "Struggle is a never-ending process. Freedom is never really won. You earn it in every generation."[4] Although you may never be able to truly undo the material implications of historical racial injustice, you can work with others in your communities to demonstrate what real healing and repair can look like.

A plaque I once saw on a wall leading into the American Church in Paris, France, boldly announced it as an "Embassy of the Kingdom of God." They were proclaiming that this church sought to represent what the spiritual realm of God looks like, inclusive of every race and culture, a place where everyone belongs. This vision is the ultimate goal of a healed and repaired community where love and acceptance are embodied in the systems, mirrored in the structures, and reflected in the values of that community. Love for our fellow human beings and love for God drive us to create this type of divine community. I always return to that love when I begin to question whether my work has been worth it.

Love for God and God's people gives me the strength to hope and empowers me to keep going when I am disappointed and feel like giving up. It is that same love that I have tried to model to my students over the years. I recently received an email from a former student who is now the executive director of a faith-based organization committed to educating, challenging, and motivating participants to respond to marginalized communities' issues and concerns. In her email she said, "You are the reason some of us who started following you around in our tender years are still Christians because you modeled what love could look like. We went in and out of faith, but a good Brenda sermon or conversation helped us remember it was never about the religious stuff and all about the love." Her email moved me to tears because every time we devise new ways to love the world, we expand our capacity for goodness and redefine the boundaries of what is possible.

My prayer is that you will find the vision to reimagine what is possible and that you will remember what success really looks like. I pray that you will not become fatigued or deterred when folks whom you are trying to help appear jaded or exhausted or uninterested, but that you will find strength in hope and power in love to keep going. I believe that you are uniquely positioned to bring hope and healing to communities that so desperately need it. I believe you have everything within you to go both deep and long in your journey to open minds and change hearts. And I pray that as you seek to help others, you yourself will be transformed, which is the truest measure of success.

As you move forward, may you have the courage and faith to disturb the comfortable and comfort the disturbed. I pray that you will be brave enough to keep asking and seeking the answers to thoughtful, relevant, and challenging questions. And may those questions lead you to become repairers of the breach and restorers of streets to live in. I leave you with this poem from Jennyann "Pie" Martinez—a sister, seeker, writer—as a sending prayer and blessing:

Different Questions

Mama asks, who gets to live?
Abuela asks, who is well and who is not?
Sister inquires, why? What would it take to be whole
    and how do we get there?

"We" only ever being all of us
We being the only way
The way we come from, the place we are, the only
    means forward

God, plant questions which grow to form refuge for
    us all
All
May the soil be rich in the ashes of our mythologies
Of competition, of either/or, of zero-sum, of you or
    me
May their smoke rise as melody drifting to the stars
Plant dreams that nourish and sustain
Plant dreams we might dare to become[5]

Acknowledgments

It is with deep gratitude that I recognize the people who encouraged and supported me during my writing process. First, I must thank Romanita Harrison, who spoke on Nehemiah at a local church, which was the initial spark of inspiration for this book. Special thanks are also due to my friend and novelist Sharisse Kimbro, who provided her flawless writing style and attention to detail that helped me write this book in a much more engaging and compelling manner. My deepest thanks go to Chloe Guillot, Daniel Hill, Nicola Patton, and David Gardiner, who read the chapters of my manuscript and gave me honest and invaluable feedback, input, and advice that greatly enhanced the quality and relevance of this book. I'm also grateful for my colleague and brilliant Old Testament scholar Sara Koenig, who shared resources with me that informed and enhanced my theological understanding of Ezra-Nehemiah.

I especially want to thank my pastor, friend, and forever "sis," Rev. Gail Song Bantum and my Quest Church family for their loving faith in my ability and persistence to write this book. I also extend my gratitude to Rev. Dr. Troy Jackson for introducing me to Dr. Marshall Ganz and the game-changing world of community organizing. In addition, I am truly grateful to my agent, Lisa Jackson, the executive vice president of Alive Literary Agency; my editor, Katelyn Beaty; project editor, Eric Salo; and the senior marketing director, Jeremy Wells, at Brazos Press for their patient, professional, and caring guidance and support throughout this writing process. A huge thank you also goes to Matt Lewis (a.k.a. Hiro) for creating this innovative and beautiful book cover and who is one of the best graphic designers I know!

In closing, my heartfelt thanks and deep appreciation goes to Carol Quinlan, the greatest executive assistant I could have ever hoped for. You are an answer to prayer, and I thank God for your excellence and ongoing partnership in ministry. I also thank my friends Roy and D'Aun Goble for their generosity and hospitality in giving me the use of their guesthouse for two weeks to focus on writing this book. It was a joy and a gift to be your writer in residence! I also thank God for my beloved dog, Bella, who was my prayer partner and walking buddy on this journey. On many occasions during our walks, the Spirit spoke to me and gave me clarity and insight into the various principles and concepts contained in this book. Finally, I am grateful for my intercessory prayer warriors—Joanne Jennings, Tom Hurley, Rick Richardson, Carol Roberts, Rosanne Swain, and Nancy Sugikawa, who believed God with me and prophetically called this book into being.

For all these good gifts and more, I sincerely give God thanks!

Notes

Preface

1, Omari McNeil, "I see the outrage and sadness," Facebook, May 7, 2020, https://www.facebook.com/omari.mcneil/posts/10163717252710464.

Introduction

1. Brenda Salter McNeil, *Roadmap to Reconciliation 2.0: Moving Communities into Unity, Wholeness, and Justice* (Downers Grove, IL: IVP Books, 2016), 26.

2. Robert Jeffress, cited in "Read the Sermon Donald Trump Heard Before Becoming President," *Time*, January 20, 2017, https://time.com/4641208/donald-trump-robert-jeffress-st-john-episcopal-inauguration.

Chapter 1: Ask the Right Questions

1. Gun Violence Archive, https://www.gunviolencearchive.org. This website is regularly updated.

2. "Explainer," Gun Violence Archive, last edited May 31, 2023, https://www.gunviolencearchive.org/explainer.

3. This quote is widely attributed to Neil Postman, but the original source is not known.

4. Carl Alviani, "The Science Behind Storytelling," *Medium*, October 11, 2018, https://medium.com/the-protagonist/the-science-behind-storytelling-51169758b22c.

5. Wes Moore, *The Other Wes Moore: One Name, Two Fates* (New York: Spiegel & Grau, 2011), 76.

6. Robert J. Schreiter, *Reconciliation: Mission and Ministry in a Changing Social Order* (Maryknoll, NY: Orbis Books, 1992), 34.

7. Schreiter, *Reconciliation*, 36.

8. Desmond Tutu, *No Future without Forgiveness* (New York: Doubleday, 1997), 165.

9. Chimamanda Ngozi Adichie, "The Danger of a Single Story," TEDGlobal, July 2009, https://www.ted.com/talks/chimamanda_ngozi _adichie_the_danger_of_a_single_story.

Chapter 2: Identify with the Plight of People

1. Cole Arthur Riley, *This Here Flesh* (New York: Convergent, 2022), 103.

2. Jemar Tisby, *The Color of Compromise* (Grand Rapids: Zondervan, 2019), 202.

3. Henri Nouwen, *The Wounded Healer: Ministry in Contemporary Society* (Garden City, NY: Doubleday, 1972), 4.

4. Howard Thurman, *Jesus and the Disinherited* (Boston: Beacon, 1996), xix.

5. Robert J. Schreiter, *Reconciliation: Mission and Ministry in a Changing Social Order* (Maryknoll, NY: Orbis Books, 1992), 36.

6. Andi Lloyd, "The Land Mourns," *Christian Century*, September 2022, https://www.christiancentury.org/article/features/land-mourns.

7. David Leong, "The Theology of a Collapsed Condo Building," *Sojourners*, July 14, 2021, https://sojo.net/articles/theology-collapsed -condo-building.

8. Cole Arthur Riley, *This Here Flesh: Spirituality, Liberation, and the Stories That Make Us* (New York: Convergent, 2022), 98.

9. Andi Lloyd, "Hosea Testifies to an Earth That Laments with Its People," *Christian Century*, September 2022, https://www.christiancen tury.org/print/pdf/node/41005.

10. Riley, *This Here Flesh*, 101.

11. "Rebekah Eklund on Practicing Lament," Calvin Institute of Christian Worship, August 22, 2022, https://worship.calvin.edu/resources /resource-library/rebekah-eklund-on-practicing-lament.

12. Chief Seattle, speech, 1854, available at https://suquamish.nsn.us /home/about-us/chief-seattle-speech.

Chapter 3: Pursue Proximity to the Problem

1. Soong-Chan Rah, foreword to *Race and Place: How Urban Geography Shapes the Journey to Reconciliation* by David Leong (Downers Grove, IL: IVP Books, 2017), 10.

Chapter 4: Organize a Diverse Coalition

1. Heather McGhee, *The Sum of Us: What Racism Costs Everyone and How We Can Prosper Together* (New York: One World, 2021), xxii.

2. Audre Lorde, *Sister Outsider: Essays and Speeches* (1984; repr., New York: Penguin, 2020), 102.

3. McGhee, *Sum of Us*, 14.

4. Martin Luther King Jr., *Where Do We Go from Here: Chaos or Community?* (Boston: Beacon, 2010), 102.

5. David Leong, *Race and Place: How Urban Geography Shapes the Journey to Reconciliation* (Downers Grove, IL: IVP Books, 2017), 36.

6. Leong, *Race and Place*, 36.

Chapter 5: Repair the Breach Together

1. Bryan Stevenson, "Questioning Ourselves and History, Talking Injustice: A Community Conversation," lecture, Seattle First United Methodist Church, Seattle, Washington, February 24, 2016, https://thechurch council.org/bryan-stevenson-speaking-in-seattle.

2. Dominique DuBois Gilliard, *Subversive Witness: Scripture's Call to Leverage Privilege* (Grand Rapids: Zondervan, 2021), 5.

3. Erin Blakemore, "The History of Book Bans—and Their Changing Targets—in the U.S.," *National Geographic*, April 24, 2023, https://www.nationalgeographic.com/culture/article/history-of-book-bans-in -the-united-states.

4. Kelly Jensen, "37 States and Millions of Students Impacted by 2022–2023 School Year Book Bans So Far: PEN America's Latest Report," Book Riot, April 20, 2023, https://bookriot.com/pen-america-book-ban -report-2023.

5. Quoted in Ariana Garcia, "Ruby Bridges Speaks Out against Texas Book Bans at Congressional Hearing," Chron, updated April 8, 2022, https://www.chron.com/politics/article/Texas-book-ban-Ruby-Bridges -desegregation-17066921.php.

6. Mark Labberton, "The Reparational God," in *Reparations and the Theological Disciplines: Prophetic Voices for Remembrance, Reckoning, and Repair*, ed. Michael Barram, Drew G. I. Hart, Gimbiya Kettering, and Michael J. Rhodes (Lanham, MD: Lexington, 2023), chap. 9.

7. Quoted in Ezra Klein, "Bryan Stevenson on How America Can Heal," Vox, July 20, 2020, https://www.vox.com/21327742/bryan-steven son-the-ezra-klein-show-america-slavery-healing-racism-george-floyd -protests.

8. Labberton, "Reparational God," 4.

9. Ta-Nehisi Coates, "'Better Is Good': Obama on Reparations, Civil Rights, and the Art of the Possible," *Atlantic*, December 21, 2016, https://www.theatlantic.com/politics/archive/2016/12/ta-nehisi-coates-obama -transcript-ii/511133.

10. Jennifer Harvey, *Dear White Christians: For Those Still Longing for Racial Reconciliation*, 2nd ed. (Grand Rapids: Eerdmans, 2020), 171.

11. Eddie Yoon, Christopher Lochhead, Dave Ferguson, and Quentin Mumphery, "Could Gen Z Consumer Behavior Make Capitalism More Ethical?," *Harvard Business Review*, December 14, 2020, https://hbr.org /2020/12/could-gen-z-consumer-behavior-make-capitalism-more-ethical.

12. Holly Williams, Barny Smith, and Tucker Reals, "One of King Charles' Relatives Pushes for U.K. Families That Profited from Slavery to Make Amends," CBS News, April 24, 2023, https://www.cbsnews.com /news/king-charles-relative-heirs-of-slavery-royal-family-transatlantic -slave-trade.

13. Lisa Weiner, "British Aristocrats Ask King Charles to Join a Slavery Reparations Movement," NPR, April 26, 2023, https://www.npr.org/2023 /04/26/1171593635/british-aristocrats-ask-king-charles-to-join-a-slavery -reparations-movement.

14. Harvey, *Dear White Christians*, 244.

Chapter 6: Expect External and Internal Opposition

1. Carla Gasser, "Lessons from Nehemiah: When Rebuilding Brings Opposition and Obstacles," Carla Gasser: At the Crossroads, July 14, 2016, https://carlagasser.com/when-rebuilding-brings-opposition-and -obstacles.

2. Michael Schaffer, "Ted Yoho, It's Been a Week and You Still Haven't Apologized for Loving Your God, Your Country, and Your Family," Washingtonian, July 28, 2020, https://www.washingtonian.com/2020/07/28/ted -yoho-aoc-wont-apologize-for-loving-god-country-and-family.

3. Her full remarks are available at Barbara Sprunt, "'I Could Not Allow That to Stand': Ocasio-Cortez Rebukes Republican for Vulgar Insult," NPR, July 23, 2020, https://www.npr.org/2020/07/23/894596598 /i-could-not-allow-that-to-stand-ocasio-cortez-rebukes-republican-for -vulgar-insu.

4. Catherine Clark Kroeger and Mary J. Evans, eds., *The IVP Women's Bible Commentary* (Downers Grove, IL: InterVarsity, 2002), 259.

5. James C. Harrington, "What Martin Luther King Jr. Learned at His Midnight Kitchen Table Experience," *Caller Times*, January 14, 2022, https://www.caller.com/story/opinion/forums/2022/01/14/what-mlk-jr -learned-his-midnight-kitchen-table-experience/6510892001; "Prayer and

Dr. Martin Luther King Jr.," GodWeb, accessed August 24, 2023, http://www.godweb.org/kingprayers.htm.

Chapter 7: Stay Covered in Prayer

1. Robert Schreiter, *The Ministry of Reconciliation: Spirituality and Strategies* (Maryknoll, NY: Orbis Books, 1998), 14.

2. Gregory Jao, "Tonight I was asked to pray at InterVarsity Live," Facebook, May 8, 2020, https://www.facebook.com/greg.jao/posts/pfbid0Q4ozzfuTsYBYE1extEekAkRcN56HeGDcGumKoLxrhqgdPerzQ395QqKPEAqowawml.

3. Michael D. Lemonick, "The Biology of Joy," *Time*, January 9, 2005, https://content.time.com/time/magazine/article/0,9171,1015863,00.html.

4. Steve Hayner and Sharol Hayner, *Joy in the Journey: Finding Abundance in the Shadow of Death* (Downers Grove, IL: InterVarsity, 2015), 140.

5. C. S. Lewis, *Letters to Malcolm: Chiefly on Prayer* (San Diego: Harvest, 1964), 93.

6. Christine Schenk, "A Prayer Guided by Love," Sisters of the Divine Savior, accessed October 2, 2023, https://www.sistersofthedivinesavior.org/pray_archive/a-prayer-guided-by-love.

Chapter 8: Avoid Faithful Exhaustion

1. Desmond Tutu, "Archbishop Desmond Tutu Reflects on Working Toward Peace," Markkula Center for Applied Ethics, https://www.scu.edu/mcae/architects-of-peace/Tutu/essay.html.

2. Resmaa Menakem, *My Grandmother's Hands: Racialized Trauma and the Pathway to Mending Our Hearts and Bodies* (Las Vegas: Central Recovery, 2017), xx.

3. Nicole Daniels, "Lesson of the Day: 'What We Know about Breonna Taylor's Case and Death,'" *New York Times*, https://www.nytimes.com/2020/09/25/learning/lesson-of-the-day-what-we-know-about-breonna-taylors-case-and-death.html.

4. Rainier Avenue Church, "Space to Breathe: Reflection Space for Racial Justice," Facebook event, August 25, 2020, https://facebook.com/events/s/space-to-breathe-reflection-sp/286262999157186/?ti=cl.

5. Menakem, *My Grandmother's Hands*, 22.

6. Audre Lorde, *A Burst of Light: And Other Essays* (Mineola, NY: Ixia, 2017), 130.

7. Kim Tran, "5 Self-Care Tips for Activists—'Cause Being Woke Shouldn't Mean Your Spirit's Broke," Everyday Feminism, April 17, 2016, https://everydayfeminism.com/2016/04/self-care-for-woke-folks.

8. Ruth Haley Barton, *Strengthening the Soul of Your Leadership: Seeking God in the Crucible of Ministry* (Downers Grove, IL: InterVarsity, 2018), 19.

9. Menakem, *My Grandmother's Hands*, 179.

Chapter 9: Leverage Access to Resources

1. Heather McGhee, *The Sum of Us: What Racism Costs Everyone and How We Can Prosper Together* (New York: One World, 2021), 11–12.

2. "Grace Lee Boggs," *Bill Moyers Journal*, June 15, 2007, https://www.pbs.org/moyers/journal/06152007/profile2.html.

3. Tom Skinner, "The U.S. Racial Crisis and World Evangelism," address, Urbana 70, University of Illinois Urbana-Champaign, available at https://urbana.org/message/us-racial-crisis-and-world-evangelism.

Conclusion

1. John Lewis, with Brenda Jones, *Across That Bridge: Life Lessons and a Vision for Change* (New York: Hyperion, 2012), 8.

2. Adam Grant (@AdamMGrant), "Meaning is about making a difference, not having an audience," Twitter, October 3, 2021, 10:27 a.m., https://twitter.com/AdamMGrant/status/1444307947891445768.

3. Daniel Barenboim, quoted in Kirsty Wark, "Daniel Barenboim: 'No One Winning Middle East Conflict,'" BBC News, August 20, 2014, https://www.bbc.com/news/av/entertainment-arts-28868318.

4. Coretta Scott King, *My Life with Martin Luther King Jr.* (Austin, TX: Holt McDougal, 1969), xiii.

5. Unpublished poem reprinted with permission from the author, Jennyann "Pie" Martinez.

BRENDA SALTER McNEIL (DMin, Palmer Theological Seminary) is a dynamic speaker, award-winning author, professor, and thought leader. She is associate professor of reconciliation studies and director of the Reconciliation Studies program at Seattle Pacific University. She is also associate pastor of preaching and reconciliation at Quest Church in Seattle, Washington. McNeil is the author of *Becoming Brave*, *Roadmap to Reconciliation*, *Roadmap to Reconciliation 2.0*, and *A Credible Witness*. She is also the coauthor of *The Heart of Racial Justice*.

Connect with Brenda:

SalterMcNeil.com

 drbrendasaltermcneil

@saltermcneil

@RevDocBrenda